IMAGES OF WALES

AROUND
PONTARDAWE

Adelina Patti (1843-1919), Baroness Cederstrom, on her way to formally open the Public Hall and Institute on 6 May 1909. She is accompanied by Mr Frank Gilbertson, Chairman of the 45-strong Public Hall and Institute Committee. A grand Patti Concert was later held in the hall where the internationally famous soprano sang *Angels Ever Bright and Fair*, *Voi Che Sapete* (*Le Nozze di Figaro*) and, as an encore, *Home Sweet Home*.

IMAGES OF WALES

AROUND PONTARDAWE

Compiled by

THE PONTARDAWE HISTORIANS

Jeff Childs, Roland Murdoch, Clive Reed,
Eurig Roberts, Eunice Williams, Gordon Williams

A view of Pontardawe steelworks bar mill in 1955 showing steel ingots being reduced into bars by use of hot mill reversing mills. Ingots were reduced in size from twelve-inch square sections down to four-inch sections by roughing and finishing mills. The mill-rolls are housed in a pair of mill-standards which have motor-driven, screw-down gearing. The bars emerge onto the run-out track after completion of the reducing operation. (Painting by D. Humphreys.)

First published in 1996 by Tempus Publishing
Reprinted 1997, 2003

Reprinted in 2013 by
The History Press
The Mill, Brimscombe Port,
Stroud, Gloucestershire, GL5 2QG
www.thehistorypress.co.uk

British Library Cataloguing in Publication Data.
A catalogue record for this book is available from the British Library.

ISBN 978 0 7524 0691 6

Typesetting and origination by
Tempus Publishing Limited
Printed in Great Britain.

Contents

Boxers at the Bryn tinplate works, *c.* 1920. After completion of the shearing, rolling, annealing, cleaning, tinning, and sorting processes, the tinned plates were packed in boxes of 56 sheets for distribution and export. Sheets would have been boxed by brand-name which denoted the type of steel or iron, the manufacturing process, tin or lead coating, or black plates. Bryn tinworks brands were 'Cennen', 'Carnedd', 'Carnedd Best', 'Illtyd', 'Brython', 'Millbrook', and 'Aber'.

Mary and her 'best friends', March 1960. From left to right: Marlene, Marian, Mary and Menna.

Foreword

As I remember it, my early childhood in Pontardawe was a blissful time when, free to roam in safety, we spent the long summer days exploring every inch of our surroundings. I trailed after my two sisters, up the Hundred Steps to the top of the Barley to dance on Elephant's Rock, then across the golf course to Llanguicke Church to gaze with reverence at the ancient stones. On baking hot days we'd climb down into the dark, exquisite beauty of Cwmdu, crossing the river on slippery stones, making our way upstream past tiny waterfalls and mossy banks. Pontardawe seemed to me a place crammed with delights – three cinemas, the park (which my father designed) with playground, paddling-pool, tennis courts, and even a bowling green for grown-ups. Life was an endless thrill of discovery. 'We're going down the village', my mother would say and, eyes level with the counter, I was treated to a feast of sights and smells at the local shops.

Ponty's most exciting industries were undoubtedly the 'pop works' and the record factory. Feasting on dandelion and burdock and Smith's crisps, we heard the hits of the day on badly scratched vinyl scavenged from the factory skip. If too far gone, we'd mould them into hideous black flowerpots – and the recycling seed was sown.

My early schooldays were a joy, first at the Infants' and then Llanguicke Girls' School, with the best ever school dinners. I adored my teachers and formed lifelong friendships. Later, at Ponty Grammar, my chief interests were music, art and boys. On special Sundays at Tabernacle, with my best friends, Marian, Marlene and Menna, angelic in our best hats and gloves, I could have sung to eternity.

It was on Sunday evenings that my grandfather, Will Hopkin, visited us. Standing shyly in line, we received a pat on the head and a butterscotch sweet. 'Diolch yn fawr, Dad.' 'Da iawn', he'd reply. Then, after a brief enquiry about our schoolwork, the Victorian ritual mercifully over, we'd dutifully kiss him on the cheek and scuttle back to our rooms. 'Dad' Hopkin had begun his career on the *Chicago Tribune* and later, in 1919, after returning to Pontardawe, he established his own successful weekly newspaper, the *West Wales Observer*.

The strong moral values we learnt while growing up in this close-knit valley community saw me safely through the superficial world of pop music. The childhood haunts, which thankfully remain unspoilt, are now cherished by my own children, who may still catch glimpses of life as it was for me in those happy, carefree days.

Mary Hopkin

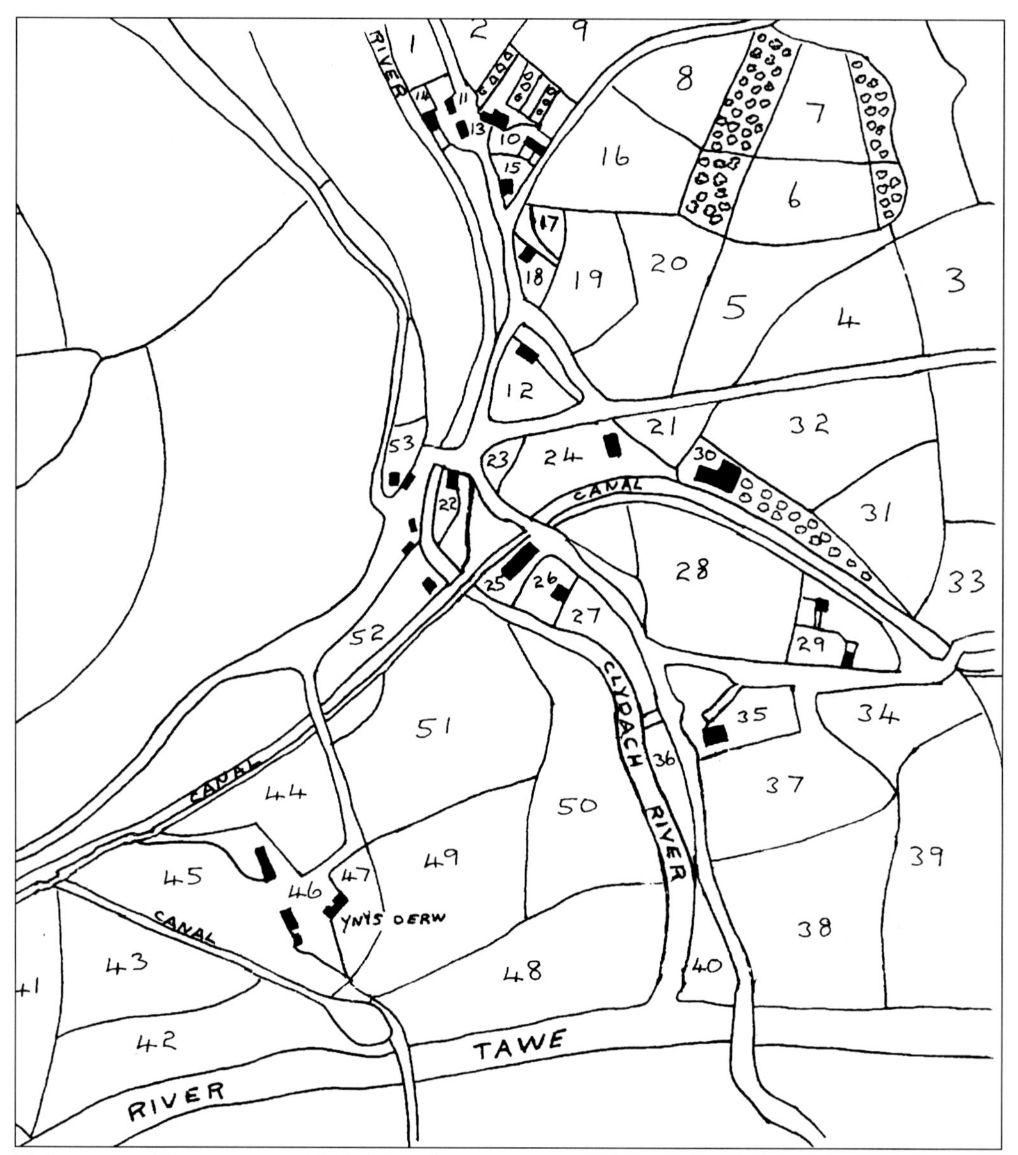

Tithe map of Pontardawe, 1838. This shows how sparsely populated the area was before the advent of heavy industry. The two ancient farmsteads of Ynysderw and Ynysygelynen (plot 35) occupied the valley floor between the River Tawe and the Swansea Canal, with the greatest part of the landscape still pasture and woodlands. Pontardawe was slowly beginning to develop around the canal. The town took its name from the bridge that spanned the River Tawe; Pont-ar-Dawe (Bridge on the Tawe). Wooden bridges were recorded at that location in 1583, 1675, and 1711, finally culminating in William Edwards' stone bridge constructed *c.* 1760.

Introduction

The focus of this photographic compilation is Pontardawe and district, the latter comprising Alltwen, Gellinudd, Cilybebyll, Rhos, Trebanos, Gellygron, Rhyd-y-fro, Ynysmeudwy and Cilmaengwyn. It seeks to capture a vivid past, rich in history and incident and represents the first book of its kind in this part of the Swansea Valley.

Geographically, the area is drained by the River Tawe and its several tributaries, the principal one being the Upper Clydach. The majority of the area lies over 500 feet reaching heights of 1,000 feet or over on broad wind-blasted summits such as Mynydd Carnllechart and Mynydd March Hywel. Other mountains in the area are Craig yr Abbey, Craig Alltwen, Craig Ynysderw, Craig Glynmeirch, Mynydd Gellionen, Craig Llangiwg, Garth, Gwrhyd and Mynydd Alltygrug.

Geologically, being situated in the western sector of the South Wales coalfield, the area is underlain by rock of the Carboniferous System, in particular the Pennant and Upper Coal Series. It is the hard Pennant sandstone, comprising as it does the chief coal seams of the district, which gives rise to the monotonous tract of moorland that dominates much of the undulating topography above the valley floor.

Historically, the area transcended four 'ancient' ecclesiastical parishes: Llangyfelach (with its hamlet of Rhyndwyglydach); Llangiwg (with its hamlets of Mawr, Blaenegel and part of Alltygrug); Cilybebyll; and Cadoxton juxta Neath (with its hamlet of Ynysymond comprising land in Alltwen and Trebanos). The boundary between Llangyfelach and Llangiwg parishes was the Upper Clydach River while the Tawe was the natural boundary dividing Cilybebyll parish from both. The Nant Llechau formed part of the boundary between Cilybebyll and Cadoxton juxta Neath parishes. In the medieval and early modern periods, Cilybebyll parish fell within the manor of Neath Ultra and Cilybebyll, part of Neath lordship. Llangyfelach and Llangiwg parishes formed the core of Gower Supraboscus, the largest component of Gower Wallicana (Welsh Gower), the northernmost part of the lordship of Gower.

The coming of 'large scale' industry in the first half of the nineteenth century saw the start of a process which was to lead to tumultuous social and economic change. One consequence of this during the course of the century was the growth of population, almost exclusively the result of inward migration. In 1851 the district's population was some 2,300; in 1891 it was some 5,650 comprising

1,800 in Pontardawe, 1,160 in Alltwen, 830 in Trebanos, 760 in Ynysmeudwy, 300 in Rhos and district, 190 in Rhyd-y-fro village and 290 in the wider Blaenegel district, 150 in Gellinudd, 90 in Cilybebyll and 80 in Cilmaengwyn. The population today is approximately 15,000.

The heavy industry which gave rise to the modern district and the influx of people (the 'Bubbs and the Suffs') has long disappeared. This book seeks to recollect that past not for sentimental reasons but because it is one intrinsically worth recounting, especially given the dramatic (some would say traumatic) and irreversible physical and topographical changes that have occurred since the demise of the steel, sheet and tinplate industries nearly 40 years ago.

Due to constraints of space it has not been possible to include every facet of the community's experience. We are very conscious, for example, that the effects of the two world wars on the district have had to be omitted. Maybe your favourite photograph or image from this or other social spheres has also not been included. We can only apologise for this but should a second volume emerge the authors would be very pleased to receive all appropriate contributions and in any event would encourage readers to loan material to any of them for a short period in order for a permanent copy to be made. Faced with the unrelenting pace of change it is essential that a photographic record of yesterday's, and indeed today's, events is kept.

'Steelworks town'. Pontardawe was dominated by its heavy industries of steel, sheet and tinplate. The works buildings, tall chimneys, smoke, noise, and smells intruded into all aspects of life in the town, as well as giving employment to 2,000 people in the community. The visual dominance of the steelworks over Pontardawe is most pronounced in this 1930s view.

One

Maps and General Scenes

The earliest cartographic depiction of Pontardawe and district appears in Emmanuel Bowen's New and Accurate Map of South Wales *of 1729 when the names 'Pont Cledach', 'Pont-ar-Dawye', 'Gallt wen' and 'Killybebill' are recorded. This information is essentially replicated in Thomas Kitchen's* Accurate Map of the County of Glamorgan *(1754). Swansea Canal maps of 1793 and 1797 show more local details, particularly the latter, which as well as delineating the road pattern in Pontardawe reveals an aqueduct, two locks, two bridges (Pontarclydach and Ynysygelynen), the town dock and wharf. In 1799, George Yates published his acclaimed* Map of the County of Glamorgan *in which Pontardawe, Alltwen, Place Killbebyll and three local farms are named – Gellygron, Ynysmeudwy (Uchaf) and Hendre Gradog. Other small-scale maps followed including the Ordnance Survey line drawings of 1813 and the first one-inch OS map of 1830. It was not until the late 1830s and 1840s that the first large-scale representations of the district appeared in the shape of the tithe maps for the ecclesiastical parishes of Llangyfelach, Llangiwg and Cilybebyll, all dated 1838. A generation or so later, the first large-scale six-inch and 25-inch OS maps were published. By then (1877/8), Pontardawe was becoming urbanised and the maps and general scenes in the following chapter show this process.*

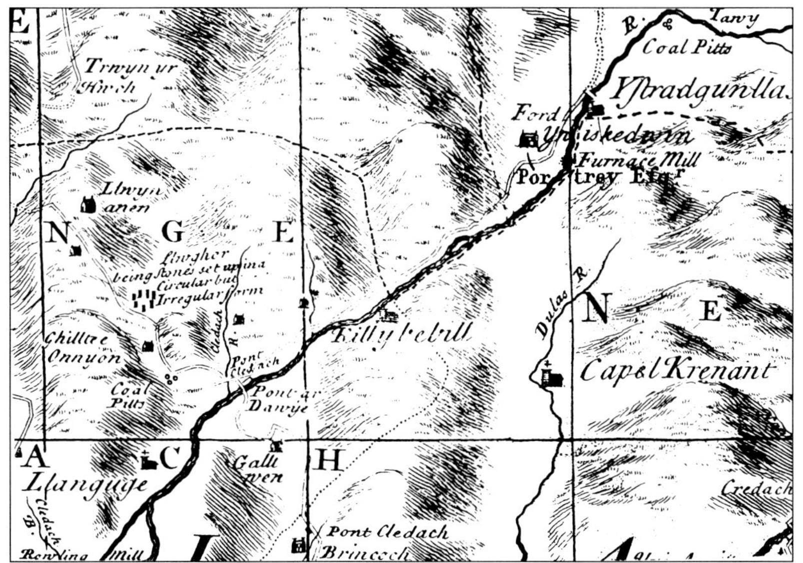

An extract from Emmanuel Bowen's *New and Accurate Map of South Wales* (1729). The map is in fact inaccurate in part, the topographical detail being the product of information received rather than a true ground survey. Note the position of 'Llanguge' church for example! The stone circle on Mynydd Carn Llechart (known to some as Cerrig Pikes) is shown. One of the most impressive Bronze Age monuments in Glamorgan, it consists of a ring of twenty-five upright slabs enclosing a central burial cist.

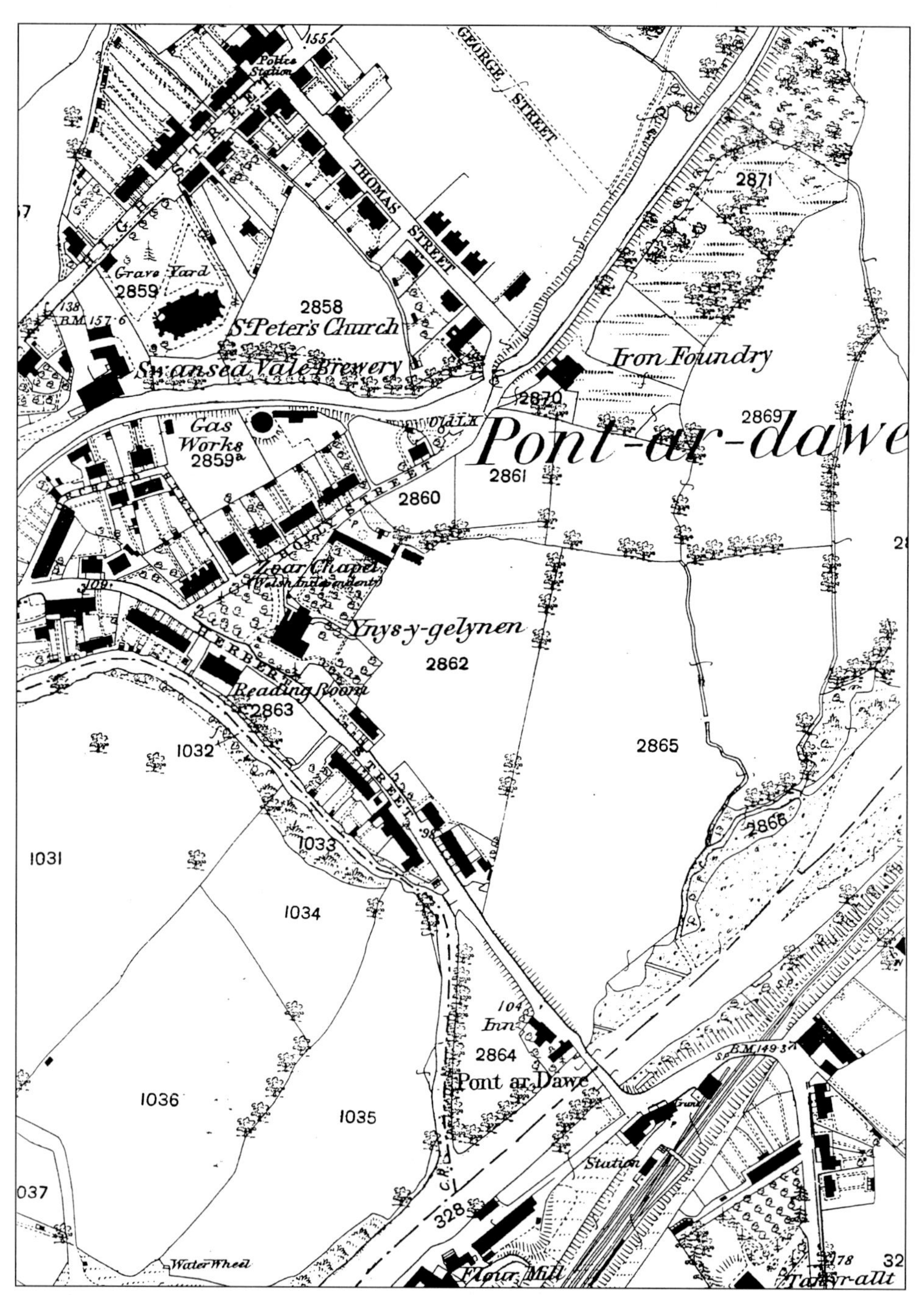

Pontardawe in 1877. Note the open fields of Ynysderw Farm (left) and Ynysygelynen (centre). Both formed part of the Cilybebyll estate. Other landmarks visible are: the police station (built 1867); St Peter's church (1860); the Swansea Vale Brewery (1837/8); the iron foundry (1865); the gas works (1869/70); Soar Chapel (1866); the reading room (1869); the Pontardawe Inn (pre-1869); the railway station (1860); the Pontardawe (flour) mill (pre-1838) and the Pontardawe Collegiate School, Tanyrallt House (1870). Thomas Street has been newly constructed and the proposed layout of George Street is shown.

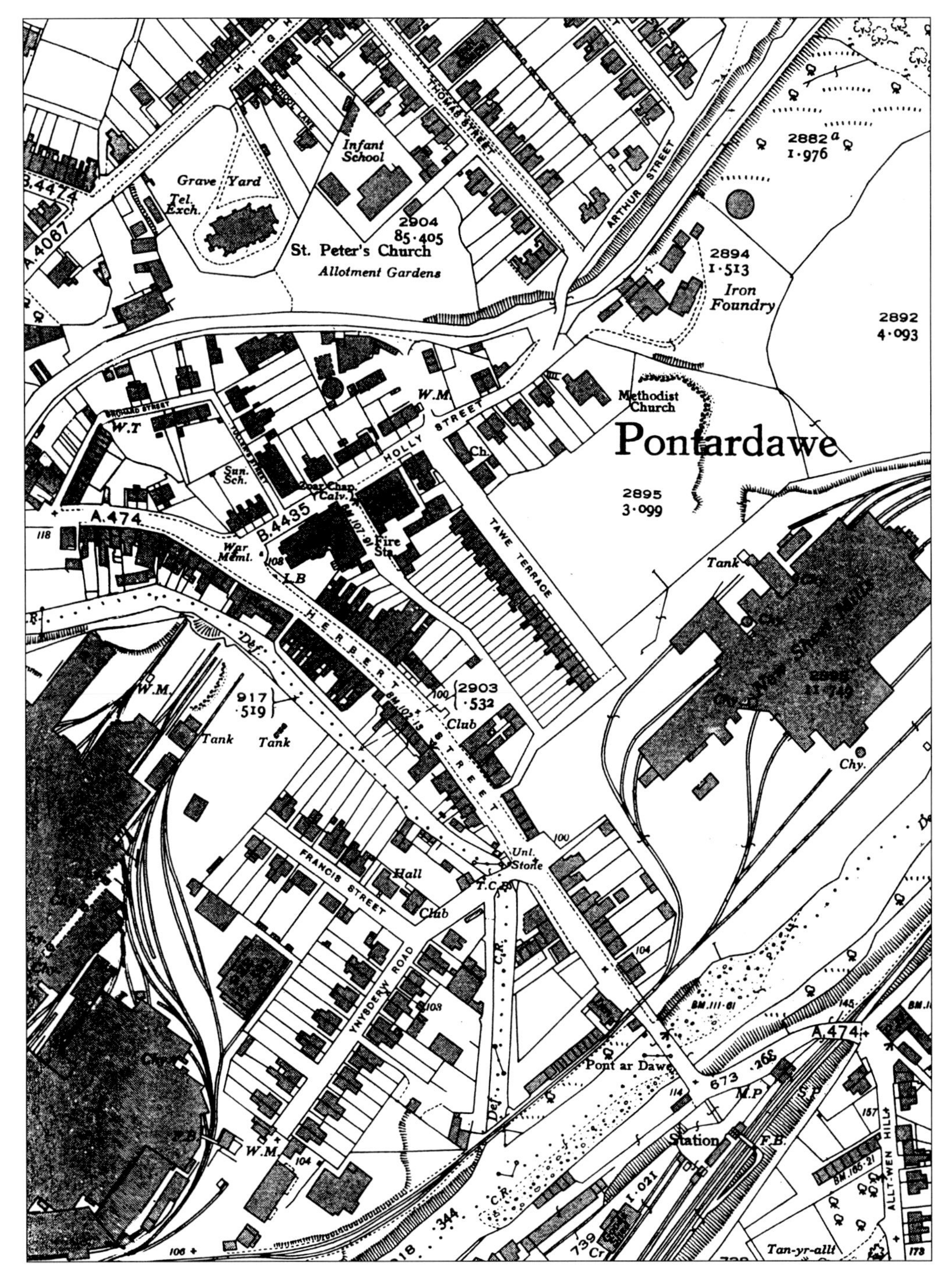

By 1942 Pontardawe had become a mature urban community. The expansion of the tinplate and steelworks on Ynysderw land is evident as is the emergence of Ynisderw Road and Francis Street. The fields of Ynysygelynen had been 'usurped' by the sheet works. Other new features were: Tawe Terrace (pre-1918); the infants school (1899); Tabernacle Chapel (1881); the war memorial (1923); the RDC (Rural District Council) offices (*c.* 1907); the fire station (pre-1941) and the English Wesleyan Methodist Church (1906).

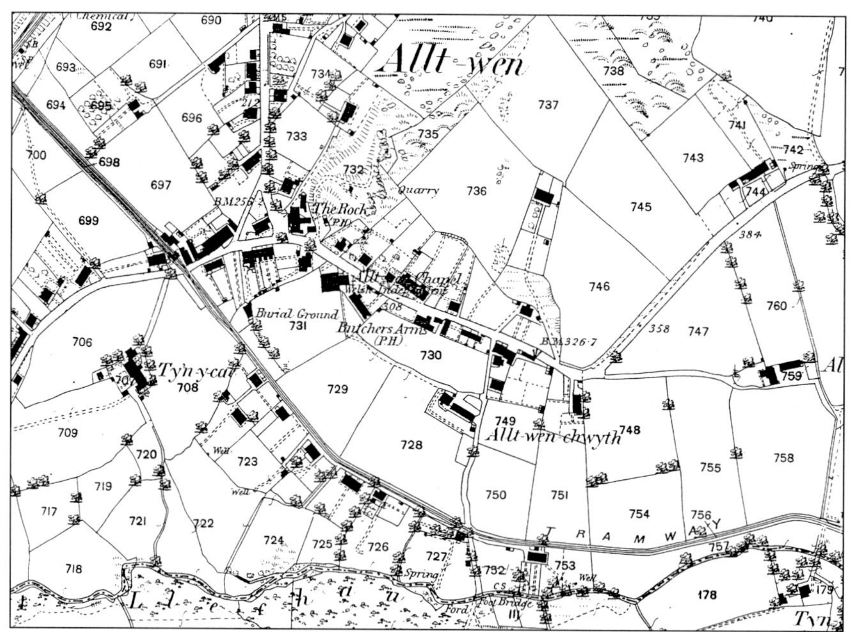

Alltwen in 1878, showing the nucleus of the community. Until 1821 all this land had been part of the Briton Ferry estate. In that year it was acquired by William Gwyn of Neath, the father of Howel. The Dramroad Incline is shown (now Lon y Wern). The tramway took coal from the Primrose Colliery, Rhos, across Gwyn Street through Alltwen Isaf land (Ynysfechan) where it abutted the chemical works, then crossed the bridge over the Tawe to be loaded on to barges on the company's branch canal, shown on the tithe map (see p. 8).

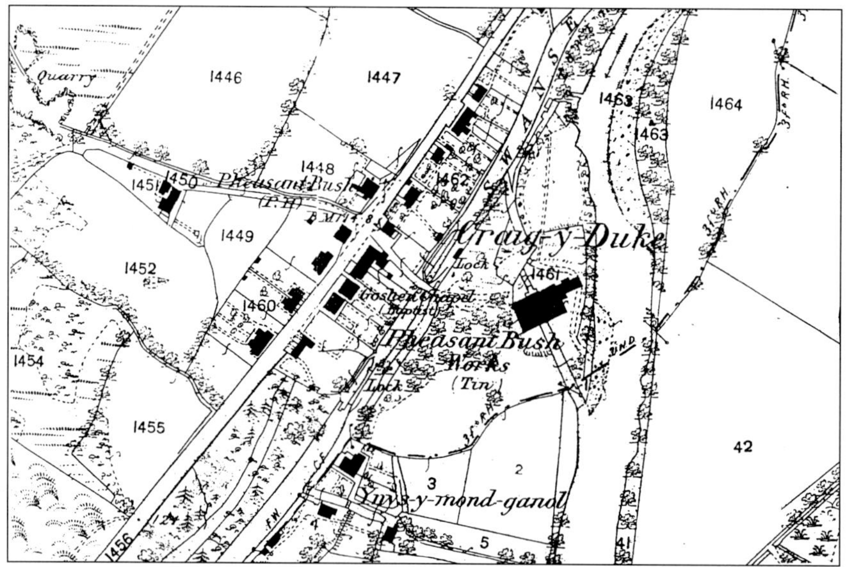

Trebanos in 1878. This was originally a farming community although coal mining had long been practised on Graig Trebanos. The population grew further following the opening of the Pheasant Bush tinplate works *c.* 1837 (closed 1893) and the Daren Colliery (*c.* 1890). Craig-y-Duke is presumably so called because it lay on Graig Trebanos land owned by the Duke of Beaufort, lord of Gower. Gosen Baptist Chapel was built in 1865. Though west of the River Tawe, Ynysymond Ganol (The Green today) lay in Cadoxton juxta Neath parish.

Pontardawe and Alltwen in early 1930s, viewed from the Barley, with Alltycham House in the foreground. An 'ancient' site, Alltycham was at one time owned by the Penllergaer estate but in 1838 Josiah Rees, son of the Arminian minister, was the owner and from c. 1853 it was in the possession of Griffith Lewis, part-owner of the Primrose Colliery. To the right is the Pontardawe Technical College and to the left Pontardawe Grammar School. In the background is The Graig, with Alltwen Hill, Graig Road, Dyffryn Road and Railway Terrace discernible.

Herbert Street from Pontardawe railway station, c. 1905, showing, on the left, the blacksmith's shop in front of the Pontardawe Inn and, a little beyond, what became James the Baker's and Arthur Evans's ironmongery. The building on the right was Midland House (drapers) in 1891 and became the Continental Cafe in the 1960s. Centre right is a rare glimpse of Ynysygelynen House (in white) which was demolished c. 1907 to make way for the Public Hall and Institute. Also partly shown is 'The Laurels' (from 1922-92 the Royal British Legion Club) and the back of No 4 Ynisderw Road.

A superb aerial shot of the steel and tinplate works and the surrounding town *c.* 1958. Note their close proximity, as well as All Saints church, Primrose Row, Compass Row, Adulum, Horeb and Soar chapels, the Rink, the Pavilion cinema, the works pond, Carpenters Row, the brewery and the gas works.

A smoky vista taken from Dyffryn Road, Alltwen, *c.* 1930. It shows Alltwen Primary School, Mill Row, the chemical works, the steel and tinplate works (and the administrative offices), Ynisderw Road, Francis Street (beyond which is the 'tennis field'), Herbert Street, the Uplands, Craig Ynysderw and Mynydd Gellionen.

'Brynheulog' and Alltycham, *c.* 1940. 'Brynheulog' (centre) was demolished in 1978/9 and the land today is covered by Bryn Derwen, Brynonnen, Bryn Gelyn, Ffordd Brynheulog, Llys Brynheulog and Hafan Brynheulog (developed from 1976). Alltycham Farm and Alltycham House are in the background and to the right are the Pontardawe Technical College and part of Bronywawr. The houses in the foreground lie along Maes Iago.

A view of Pontardawe overlooking Dynevor Terrace and Church Street, 1904. Quarr Road, Jones Street and Hopkin Street were still to be developed (they lay on Dynevor Arms land) and Horeb Chapel is still to be built. Note the Pontardawe Telephone Exchange (where Barclays Bank is today) which had been established in 1886, the partly hidden Gravel Bank House (in white), the brewery, Davies the ironmongers and, in the distance, Ynysmeudwy Isaf and Ynysmeudwy Ganol farms.

The remnant of Ynysygelynen fields, *c.* 1910 – Caer Efel and Caer Bont in 1838 – on which the sheetworks was later built. Tawe Terrace is in the course of being planned. Note the foundry, the English Wesleyan Methodist Chapel in Holly Street (now closed), the infants school, Tabernacle and, top right, the Vicarage (built 1870). The open fields of Alltycham Farm are also conspicuous.

Pontardawe from Dyffryn Road, early 1930s, with Tawe Terrace and the sheetworks now in place. Note the extent of the foundry in this shot, the position of the gasometer (later located in Holly Street) and the planned route of Bronywawr.

Two

Farms

Before the coming of heavy industry, farming formed the bedrock of the area's economy and society and remains important today. In the mid-nineteenth century the district had over 120 farms, some fifty-seven in the three Llangiwg parish hamlets of Mawr (35), Blaenegel (15) and (the Cilmaengwyn portion) of Alltygrug (7). Sixty-five farms were in those parts of Rhyndwyglydach hamlet (35) and Cilybebyll parish (30) which fall within the ambit of this study while a few such as Cilhendre Fawr and Fach and Ynysymond Ganol lay in Cadoxton juxta Neath parish. Many of the farms are of pre-1650 origin as is evident from the Gower manorial survey of that year while other records testify to an even older vintage (Cefn Celfi 1493 and Penllwynteg 1528).

Within the local agricultural economy, pastoral farming was, and is, predominant, the emphasis being on cattle and sheep rearing. There are extensive areas of moorland in the upland regions of Rhyndwyglydach and Blaenegel notably Mynydd Gellionen, Mynydd Carnllechart (otherwise Baran mountain), Garth, Gwrhyd and Penllerfedwen. The area is generally unconducive to arable cultivation as the area under grass is frequently too wet, clayey or infertile to plough. The chief crops comprise grass, barley, oats, wheat, potatoes, beans and peas. Of the land given over to arable crops in 1800, fifty per cent was devoted to oats in the parishes of Llangiwg and Cilybebyll with some thirty per cent planted with barley.

The largest landowners in the district in 1840 were Henry Leach of Plâs Cilybebyll (2,100 acres), Richard Douglas Gough of Ynyscedwyn (1,400 acres), Howel Gwyn of Neath, Baglan House and later Dyffryn Clydach (1,100 acres) and Jenkin Davies Berrington of Swansea (700 acres).

Ynysmeudwy Ganol, 1925. In 1838, this eighty-five acre farm was owned by Jenkin Davies Berrington, a notable Swansea solicitor, and was occupied by Thomas Williams. It contained twenty-three fields and was bounded by Ynysmeudwy Isaf, Ynysmeudwy Uchaf and (in small part) by Llwynmeudwy Isaf and Gellyfowy Ganol. Last occupied in 1954 by Iris Griffiths, the remains of the house were demolished in June 1987. The Swansea Valley trunk road now runs through the land.

Alltyfanog ('Boghill'). Colloquially known as 'The Allt' this farm comprised 191 acres in 1838 when owned by the Revd Thomas Gronow whose father, William, of Court Herbert, Neath, acquired it in 1821 from the Briton Ferry estate; he also owned the adjoining Cefn Eithrim Uchaf, Ganol and Isaf. One of the oldest of the Rhyndwyglydach farms, it was, along with Ynyspenllwch, Llachard and Ynysderw, one of the four 'ancient houses' described by the topographer, Rice Merrick, in 1578. It was last occupied *c.* 1963. Gwernllwyn and Eithrym Uchaf also adjoin the property.

Plasnewydd. Sixty-nine acres in 1838 when it formed part of the Ynyspenllwch estate, this was one of fourteen farms owned by the Miers family in the area. Like Ynyspenllwch it had previously been part of the Gnoll estate, Neath, owned by the Evanses and Mackworths. The present house, in the distance, was built *c.* 1900. The old house, in the foreground, is severely dilapidated and now used for storage. The adjoining farms are Gellionen Uchaf, Eithrym Uchaf and Penygraig.

Ty'n-y-Pant, c. 1900. The present house, built in the 1920s, is close to the one shown here which was the former home-farm of the Gilbertsons' Glanrhyd estate. The old property has fallen into decay though its thatched roof is still prominent. Owned by John Phillip Jones in 1838 when the farm covered fifty-nine acres, in the 1770s it was in the possession of George Ace, a member of a notable Swansea family. It was bounded in 1838 by the Graig Trebanos sheepwalk, Mynydd Gellionen, Penlan, Glynmeirch and Ynysderw farms.

Llachard Fawr. Formerly part of the Briton Ferry estate it was sold to the Jones family in 1821, Howell Jones being the owner of this 186 acre property in 1838. It subsequently became part of the Glynmeirch estate and was occupied up to the early 1980s. Like Alltyfanog, Nantymoel Uchaf and Llwyn Evan it was a dissenting meeting house, Howel Harris the Methodist evangelist, visiting the property at Christmas 1738. It is bounded by Llachard Fach, Cwmbryn, Heol Ddu and Mynydd Gellionen.

Nantymoel Uchaf. In 1838, this farm covered sixty-nine acres and was owned by the Revd Roger Howel, the minister at Baran Chapel, whose ancestors had been there since at least 1744. The house seen here was a rebuilding of 1803 and was part-used as a school in the 1820s. The farm is today owned by the Lloyd family who also farm the adjoining Pen yr Esgyrn (demolished *c.* 1963), Brynchwith (demolished *c.* 1970) and land previously forming part of Tyn Berth. Nantymoel Isaf also abuts the property.

Fforch Egel. The name derives from the forking of the Egel streams at this place. It was 223 acres in extent in 1838 when it was owned by David Davies and bounded by Bogel Egel, Blaenegel Fawr and Fach, Penywaun and Cefn Gwrhyd. There was a chapel at Fforchegel which survived for most of the eighteenth century and served the Gellionen and Cwmllynfell Independent congregations. The chapel is said to have had a graveyard but the only discernible evidence of this is the large gravestone shown standing by the front door. The worn inscription reads: 'Here lieth the body of Mary Jones (?) Bevan, the wife of Llewelyn Bevan of Ystradown [Ystradowen] Minister of the Gospel of Jesus Christ who departed this life on the 23 day of the 11 month 1724'.

Cefn Celfi, *c*. 1960. There is a reference to this farm as 'Roos Kevn-Kel-Vie' as early as 1493. The name means 'the ridge of the standing stones' which lie in the fields below the farm and have been identified with gravestones of Welsh warriors mentioned in ninth or tenth century *englyns* or stanzas. Only two of the original three stones survive but their tops have been destroyed apparently by the custom of dynamiting at special events such as the striking of coal at the Primrose Colliery or at wedding celebrations! The farm was 225 acres in 1838 and was owned by John Bruce Pryce of Duffryn Aberdare and Duffryn St Nicholas.

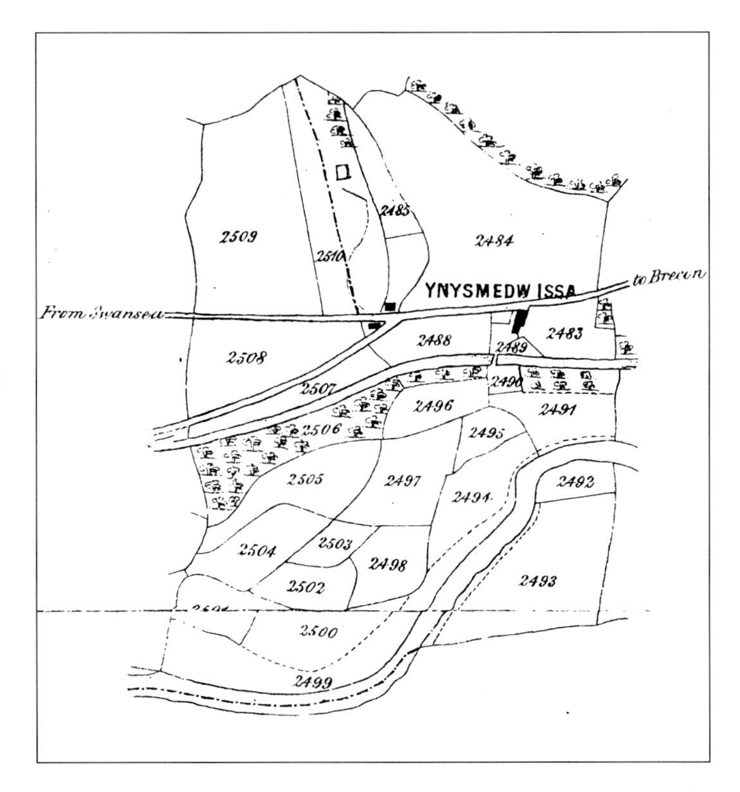

The eighty-seven acre Ynysmeudwy Isaf Farm when advertised for sale in October 1872. The farmstead is plot 2489. Though not part of the farm the larger of the two properties, shown above the forking of the Swansea to Brecon road with what later became Grove Road, was in recent times partly occupied by 'Des the Butcher'. Plots 2494 to 2505 were later developed as recreational grounds. Plots 2492 and 2493 were to be occupied by the Glantawe tinplate works. The majority of plot 2484 became the site of the workhouse while Smithfield, Oakfield and Heathfield were to be developed on plot 2509.

1923

PONTARDAWE, SWANSEA VALLEY
GLAMORGANSHIRE.

The Glynmeirch Estate

Comprising a total area of nearly 300 Acres.

Particulars, Plans & Conditions of Sale
OF THE ABOVE MENTIONED

FREEHOLD ESTATE

comprising

2 Splendid Farms, Accommodation Fields & Woodlands, Ground Rents and Building Sites

AND

18 Dwelling Houses and Cottages

which will be offered for Sale by Auction by

MESSRS JAMES & JAMES, F.A.I

in conjunction with

MR T. V. WILLIAMS, P.A.S.I.

(Under instructions from the Trustees of the Estate) at

The PUBLIC HALL & INSTITUTE, PONTARDAWE

On THURSDAY, NOVEMBER 29th, 1923.

in the following or such other Lots as may be decided upon prior to or at the Sale (and Subject to such Conditions of Sale as shall then and there be produced).

SALE PROMPTLY AT 5 O'CLOCK P.M.

For Further Particulars and Conditions of Sale apply to the AUCTIONEERS, 10 Portland Street, Swansea and 1. Holly Street, Pontardawe; or to the Solicitors, Messrs. R. & C. B. JENKINS & LLOYD, Fisher Street, Swansea; R. A. JONES, Esq., York Street, Swansea and Clydach; and ARTHUR HOPKINS, Esq., High Street, Pontardawe.

ALL MINES AND MINERALS ARE RESERVED.

Please bring these Particulars with you to the Sale.

Sale of Glynmeirch Farm, 1923. Glynmeirch ('the valley of the stallions') was previously a part of the Nydfwch estate and, from 1750, Penllergaer. In 1808, the farm came into the possession of the John (alias Jones) family in whose ownership it remained until 1923. Isaac Jones also acquired Llachard Fawr in 1821 which also featured in the 1923 sale (the dwelling houses were on Glynmeirch Road). It was 118 acres in 1838 and bounded by Ty'n-y-Pant, Penlan and Ynysderw. It is fifty-two acres today, much of the difference being accounted for by the sale of land to Arthur Gilbertson for the establishment of the Glanrhyd estate between 1877 and 1879.

Three

Transport

The earliest means of communication for vehicles in the Swansea Valley was along parish roads. The two major routes were the roads from Neath to Llandeilo crossing the bridge 'Pont-ar-Dawe', and the road from Swansea to Hen-Neuadd (Abercraf), and ultimately Brecon, by way of the bridge 'Pont-ar-Clydach' (Pontardawe Cross). The bridge over the River Tawe eventually gave its name to the town of Pontardawe which developed close by in the nineteenth century. Prior to the construction of the stone bridge by William Edwards in the eighteenth century, a timber bridge spanned the river at that location, and before that a ford would have existed for the movement of cattle. The parish roads were upgraded by the turnpike trusts. The Twrch Turnpike Trust (1806) improved the road between Swansea and the River Twrch and constructed High Street and Brecon Road to by-pass the winding track along what is present-day Herbert Street, Holly Street, and Grove Road. The Ynysderw Gatehouse at Trebanos still stands, the only survivor of several turnpike gates in the Pontardawe area. The road from Gwaun-Cae-Gurwen to Neath passing through Cwmgors, Rhyd-y-fro, Pontardawe, and Alltwen was improved in 1817. Turnpike Trust boundary stones can be observed today at Bryncoch, Alltwen, Pontardawe, and Rhyd-y-fro.

The Swansea Canal was constructed from Swansea to Hen-Neuadd (Abercraf) between 1794 and 1798 and had reached Pontardawe by 1796. The canal enabled the mineral resources of the valley such as coal and iron to be exploited to the full. The first major industries to emerge around the Pontardawe area were coal mining at Cilybebyll and Alltwen followed by iron and tinworks at Ynysderw. The railways were a later phase of the transport revolution to enter the valley and arrived at Pontardawe in the middle of the nineteenth century. The Swansea Vale Railway Company initially completed the line from Swansea to Pontardawe in 1859 before extending the track to colliery workings at Waun Coed and Ynysgeinon (1861), and finally Brynamman (for mineral traffic) in 1864. The most recent major improvement for transport in the area has been the Swansea Valley trunk road (A 4067), completed in 1992, which by-passes the town centres of Clydach and Pontardawe as well as Ynysmeudwy.

Swansea Canal maintenance boat, 1925. Boats on the Swansea Canal did not usually have cabins. However, the maintenance boats operated by the canal company had limited cabin space for the safe storage of tools and equipment required for the daily maintenance of the canal, towpath, fences, and stone structures along the waterway. Note the pile of branches in the boat from the cutting down of overhanging trees. George Holloway, known to past Pontardawe residents as 'Georgie Canal' is standing in the boat. Jack Phillips, the canal foreman, wearing the trilby hat, is pulling the boat along with Thomas Gwynn John (at the rear) and William Penhale (centre).

Swansea Canal boat at Ynysmeudwy, 1951. Boats on the Swansea Canal were all 64 feet long, 7 ½ feet wide, and carried 22 tons of cargo when fully laden. This particular boat is of late construction, probably about 1910. She was built with an elm bottom and angle-iron side frames, and planked with pitch-pine on the iron frames. Earlier boats would have been constructed entirely of timber. The two iron hoops visible at one end of the boat supported corrugated steel sheets which served as a cabin covering when the boat was converted to a maintenance boat. This boat was the last canal craft to pass through Ynysmeudwy Locks in 1943.

Lock 10 at Pontardawe, 1949. A survey commissioned by the Inland Waterways Association in 1949 showed that 90 per cent of the Swansea Canal was intact at that time. The two locks at Pontardawe still had workable lock gates. These locks, Nos 10 and 11, were named the Ynysderw locks. Lock 10 was 7 miles, 18 chains from Swansea, approximately half-way between the canal basins at Swansea and Hen-Neuadd (Abercraf), and raised the canal 9 feet. In the above picture, the lock entrance has been repaired in brick after damage to the stonework by boat traffic. The whole lock was demolished in the 1960s.

Upper Clydach aqueduct, Pontardawe, 1967. This was one of the four single-arch aqueducts along the line of the Swansea Canal. Constructed between 1794 and 1796, it carried the canal over the Upper Clydach River. No water is escaping over the spillway that normally allowed excess canal water to overflow into the river. The spillway has been blocked off with stop-planks to ensure all water that flowed down the canal channel was going to industries along the canal. The cottages adjacent to the aqueduct were the first row of terraced houses to be built in Pontardawe *c.* 1830. One of the cottages was converted into a public house – the Carpenters Arms (*c.* 1840) – and the row of dwellings was named Carpenters Row.

The Swansea Canal at Ynysderw lock, 1965. This backdrop of St Peter's church against an idyllic, wild-plant-filled waterway was one of the losses suffered by Pontardawe during the 1960s. The canal flowed through Ynysderw fields, later the site of heavy industry. The bridge was given the name of Works Bridge by generations of workmen who passed over the structure to gain entry to the ironworks, tinplate works and steelworks. Beyond the bridge was lock 11 and above the lock was the site of the Ynysderw dry docks where canal boats were constructed until 1920. St Peter's church was founded by the ironmaster William Parsons who created the first heavy industry at the Ynysderw Boilerplate and Tinplate Works in 1835.

Pontardawe Bridge. The first bridges at this location were of timber construction and are mentioned in leases dated 1583, 1675, and 1711. The first known mention of a bridge is in a lease of 1583 which refers to a piece of land as 'Tir Pen-y-Bont-ar-Dawe' ('The land above the bridge on the Tawe'). The present stone bridge was designed and erected by William Edwards c. 1760. This was originally constructed with circular holes in the arches to lighten the weight of the structure. The large building alongside the bridge is the Pontardawe Inn and the smaller buildings, blacksmith shops.

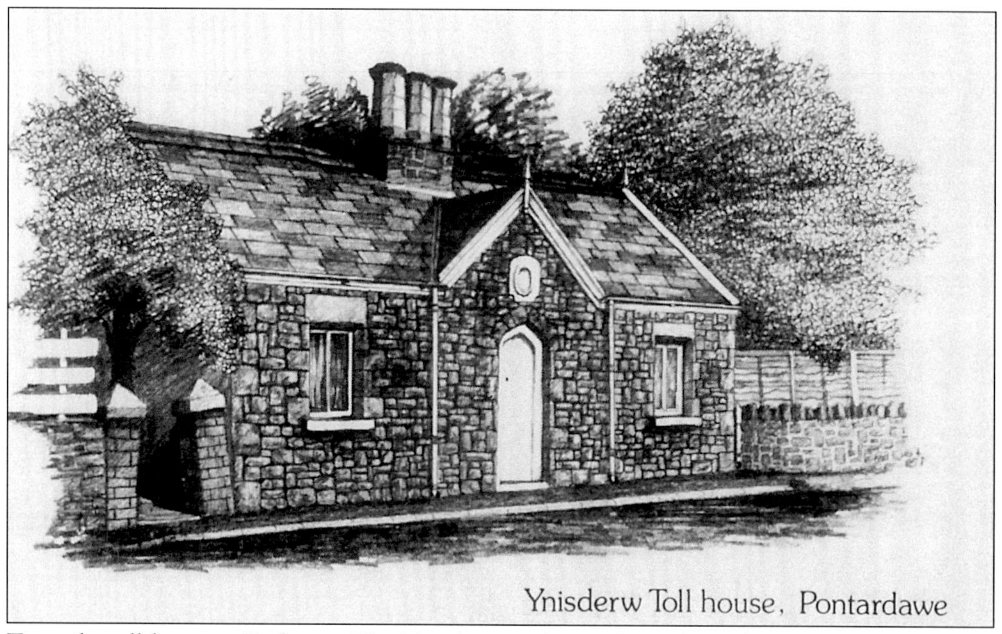

Turnpike toll-house at Trebanos. The Twrch turnpike-road ran along the Swansea Valley from Swansea to the River Twrch. There were several turnpike gates along the road of which the Ynysderw Gatehouse at Trebanos is the sole surviving example. The gatehouse was erected c. 1805 to charge tolls for using the turnpike-road. In 1861, one Charles Davies was the turnpike gate-keeper taking the tolls. A milestone alongside the gatehouse records the distance from Swansea as eight miles.

Humphreys' Garage, Swansea Road, 1940s. Started by David Humphreys, a rollerman in the Pontardawe tinplate works, and his three sons Tommy, Emlyn and Philip, some seventy years ago, it traded initially as D. Humphreys & Sons, Western Garage, and later as Philip Humphreys and Co. The premises was sold in 1982 to Brian E. Duggan, funeral director, the present occupier of the site. As well as maintaining the ambulance for W. Gilbertson and Co., the garage also provided a driver and supplied the works with petrol. It also had a wedding car and funeral business and undertook traditional vehicle repairs and maintenance for the community.

Lewis Brothers, Pontardawe, mineral water manufacturers established in 1899. The business was founded by Nathaniel Lewis who had worked for David Bevan brewers of Neath. He transferred to Pontardawe brewery and worked there for many years before founding Lewis Bros. The photograph shows a delivery lorry on Grove Road, Pontardawe, about 1910, possibly the occasion of the purchase of a new lorry. Sitting in the driver's seat is John Parker Lewis, in the centre is Mr Bishop, with Tom Lewis, brother of John, on his left. The wagon carries eighty-four standard size 'pop' boxes, each holding a dozen bottles. Lewis's also had another bottling plant at Ammanford.

Pontardawe Rural District Council electricity department staff with a new Thorneycroft lorry, 1947. Eric Buttress, the lorry driver, is by the cab-front and Bill Mason, charge-hand of the cable-laying gang, is standing, centre. The lorry door-panel carries the name of the electrical engineer Mr R.M. Jenkins. In 1935, Pontardawe RDC was advertising twenty-five hours of light for 2d and an electric iron for 12/6. The electricity department was nationalised on 1 April 1948 and became part of the South Wales Electricity Board (SWEB).

South Wales Transport Co. Ltd's bus garage on Brecon Road. The bus depot was established in 1928 and closed in 1960. The Brecon Road site lay on Caer Efel, part of the former Ynysygelynen Farm. Planning permission for the new 9,500 sq ft Tawe Terrace depot, to accommodate 24 omnibuses, was given in 1958 and building work commenced in September 1959. Eynons' Bakery now occupies the former bus depot building.

Pontardawe railway station, *c.* 1910. The Swansea Vale Railway Company (chairman, Starling Benson of Swansea) commenced a passenger service from Swansea to Pontardawe on 20 February 1860. It was extended to Ynysgeinon on 21 January 1861, Ystalyfera on 20 November 1861 and Brynamman in March 1868. It linked with Brecon via Coelbren on 20 November 1873. The Midland Railway Company bought the company in 1876 and this opened up connections to Hereford and Birmingham. It became part of the London, Midland & Scottish Railway Company (LMS) in 1923.

Pontardawe station staff pictured, *c.* 1906, at the station in front of Midland and Cambrian Railways posters depicting examples of the wide variety of possible destinations available.

Last day on the railway. Passenger trains ceased to run further than Ynysgeinon on 1 January 1931. The last scheduled passenger train for Swansea left on 20 September 1950 and the last special excursion train 'Y Glyn Crwydryn', seen here, ran in 1964. The Swansea Valley trunk road follows the course of the railway today.

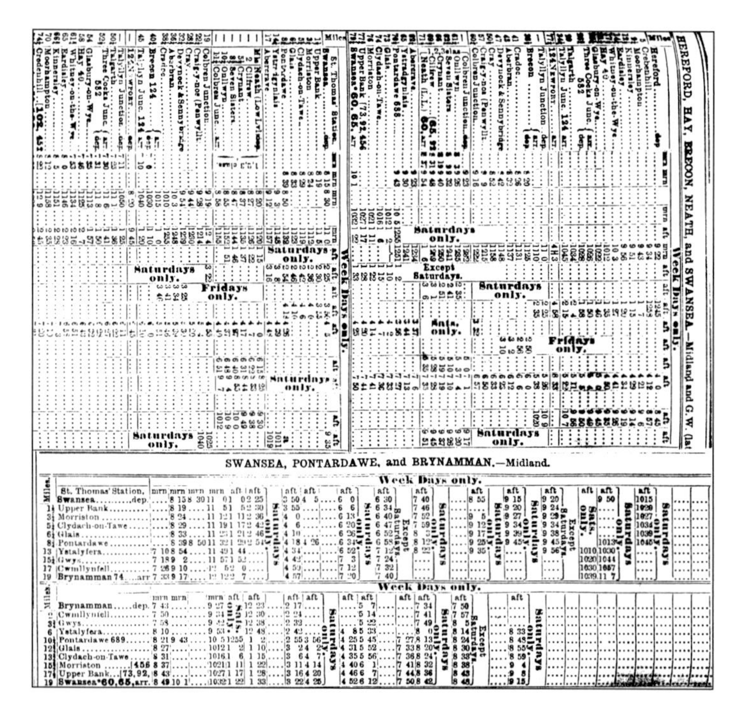

HEREFORD, HAY, BRECON, NEATH, and SWANSEA.—Midland and G. W.

SWANSEA, PONTARDAWE, and BRYNAMMAN.—Midland.

Week Days only.

Miles		mrn	mrn	mrn	mrn	aft	aft (Saturdays only)	aft	aft	aft (Saturdays only)	aft (Except Saturdays)	aft (Saturdays only)	aft (Saturdays only)	aft (Saturdays only)	aft (Except Saturdays)	aft (Sats. only)	aft (Saturdays only)	aft (Saturdays only)
	St. Thomas' Station, Swansea........dep.	....	8 15	8 30	11 0	1 0	2 25	3 50	4 5	6 0	6 30	7 40	8 55	9 15	9 20		9 50	10 15
1¼	Upper Bank	....	8 19	....	11 5	1 5	2 30	3 55	....	6 6	6 34	7 46	....	9 20	9 24		....	10 20
3¼	Morriston	....	8 24	....	11 12	1 11	2 36	4 0	....	6 13	6 40	7 52	9 5	9 27	9 29		....	10 27
5¼	Clydach-on-Tawe	....	8 29	....	11 19	1 17	2 42	4 6	....	6 20	6 47	7 59	9 12	9 34	9 34		....	10 34
6¼	Glais	....	8 33	....	11 23	1 21	2 46	4 10	....	6 26	6 52	8 3	9 17	9 39	9 38		....	10 39
8¼	Pontardawe	....	8 39	8 50	11 32	1 29	2 54	4 18	4 26	6 34	6 58	8 12	9 25	9 45	9 45		10 13	10 45
13	Ystalyfera	7 10	8 54	....	11 49	1 44	....	4 34	....	6 52	7 12	8 22	9 35	....	9 56	10 10	10 30	....
15¼	Gwys	7 18	9 2	....	11 57	1 52	....	4 42	....	7 3	7 24	....	....	....	....	10 20	10 44	....
17	Cwmllynfell	7 26	9 10	....	12 5	2 0	....	4 50	....	7 12	7 32	....	....	....	....	10 30	10 57	....
19	Brynamman 74....arr	7 33	9 17	....	12 12	2 7	....	4 57	....	7 20	7 40	....	....	....	....	10 39	11 7	....

Week Days only.

Miles		mrn	mrn	mrn	aft (Sats. only)	aft	aft (Saturdays only)	aft (Saturdays only)	aft	aft	aft	aft (Saturdays only)	aft (Except Saturdays)	aft (Saturdays only)
	Brynamman.....dep.	7 43	....	9 27		12 23	2 17	....	....	5 7	....	7 34	7 50	....
2	Cwmllynfell	7 50	....	9 34		12 30	2 24	....	....	5 14	....	7 41	7 57	....
3¼	Gwys	7 58	....	9 42		12 38	2 32	....	....	5 22	....	7 49	8 5	....
6	Ystalyfera	8 10	....	9 53		12 48	2 42	....	4 8	5 33	....	8 0	8 14	8 33
10¼	Pontardawe 689	8 21	9 43	10 5	12 55	1 2	2 55	3 56	4 25	5 45	7 27	8 13	8 24	8 43
12¼	Glais	8 27	....	10 12	1 2	1 10	3 2	4 2	4 31	5 52	7 33	8 20	8 30	8 55
13¼	Clydach-on-Tawe	8 31	....	10 16	1 6	1 15	3 6	4 7	4 35	5 56	7 36	8 24	8 33	8 59
15¼	Morriston.......456	8 37	....	10 21	1 11	1 22	3 11	4 14	4 40	6 1	7 41	8 32	8 38	9 4
17¼	Upper Bank...73, 92,	8 43	....	10 27	1 17	1 28	3 16	4 20	4 46	6 7	7 44	8 36	8 43	9 8
19	Swansea*60, 65, arr.	8 49	10 1	10 32	1 22	1 33	3 22	4 25	4 52	6 12	7 50	8 42	8 48	9 15

A page from the 1922 Bradshaw's *Railway Guide*. Three trains a day went to Brecon and Hereford; nine trains per weekday went to Swansea and twelve on Saturdays. Note the morning express only took eighteen minutes!

Four

Iron, Tinplate and Steel

Pontardawe is not generally thought of as a 'tinopolis' to rival the ranks of Llanelli, Pontarddulais and Morriston, yet it was a tinplate town par excellence. *Four works were established in the district, the first being an ironworks in 1835 to be followed by a tinplate and boiler plate manufactory, both built on Ynysderw Farm land. Mills were also erected at Trebanos c. 1837 (the Pheasant Bush works). The Ynysmeudwy (later the Bryn) tinplate works was built in 1879 on the site of the former Ynysmeudwy brickworks and pottery. The Glantawe tinplate works was also erected in 1879 and renamed the Glanrhyd works in 1883, having been acquired by Arthur Gilbertson and it was under the direction of this family that the greatest advances took place in the manufacture of tinplate, steel and galvanised sheet in the late nineteenth and early twentieth centuries. By the late 1930s, most of what had been Ynysderw Farm land had been taken up by steel and tinplate manufacture while on the fields of what had been Ynysygelynen Farm, new sheet mills were erected in 1921 on land known as the Alloy since 1918 (see map on p. 13).*

While the nature of the work in the steel and tinplate works forged teamwork and communal solidarity the work itself was extremely arduous, the wages hardly compensating for the 'heat, exertion and all pervading stife'. The rollermen, doublers, behinders, annealers and picklers of the tinplate works have, like the front-line workers of the steelworks (those employed in the bar and billet mills, casting pit and melting shop), passed into folklore. All that remains of the industrial complex on the Ynysderw site today is part of the former tinplate manufactory and the administrative offices. (The latter is today Ty Mawr, a sheltered housing complex.) The electric shop was standing until recently but the melting shop, casting pit, bar mill, billet mill, oil stores, carpenter's shop, blacksmith's shop, wagon shop, loco shed, laboratories, general stores, 'scruff house', time office, surgery, drawing office and canteen have long gone. Nothing of the old industry remains on the Bryn, Glanrhyd, Alloy and Pheasant Bush sites.

William Parsons, industrialist and benefactor. Born in Neath in 1797, he was an ironmaster like his father, Richard, and brother, John, and established tinplate manufactories at Pontardawe and Trebanos in the 1830s. He built Ynysderw House in the 1850s and gave generously to education and the church in the locality. Parsons sold the Pontardawe tinplate works to William Gilbertson in 1861. He died at Clifton in 1864 and is buried, together with his wife, Mary, in St Peter's church which he founded.

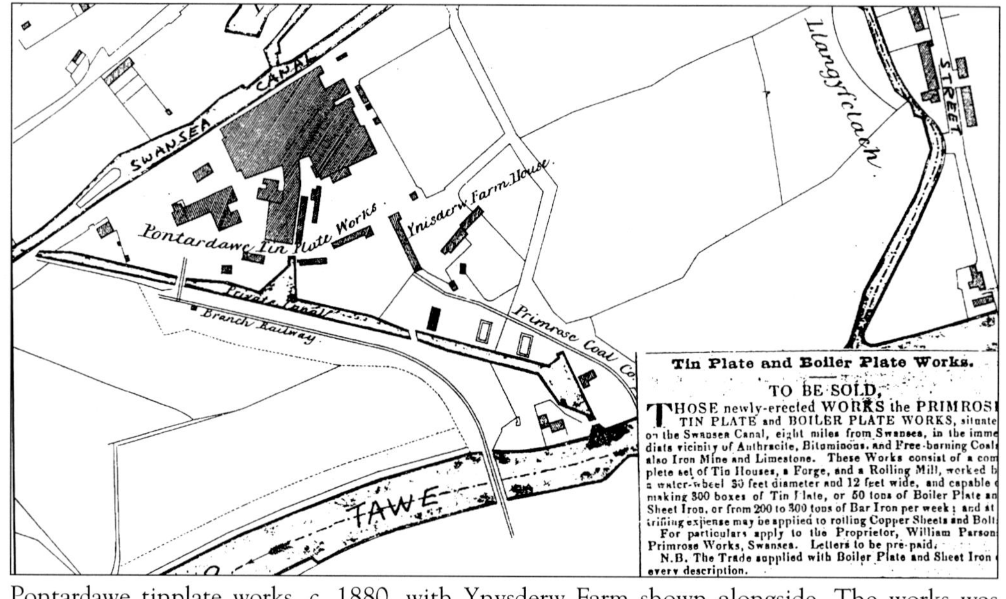

Tin Plate and Boiler Plate Works.

TO BE SOLD,

THOSE newly-erected WORKS the PRIMROS
TIN PLATE and BOILER PLATE WORKS, situate
on the Swansea Canal, eight miles from Swansea, in the imme
diate vicinity of Anthracite, Bituminous, and Free-burning Coals
also Iron Mine and Limestone. These Works consist of a com
plete set of Tin Houses, a Forge, and a Rolling Mill, worked b
a water-wheel 30 feet diameter and 12 feet wide, and capable
making 300 boxes of Tin Plate, or 50 tons of Boiler Plate an
Sheet Iron, or from 200 to 300 tons of Bar Iron per week; and at
trifling expense may be applied to rolling Copper Sheets and Bolt
For particulars apply to the Proprietor, William Parson
Primrose Works, Swansea. Letters to be pre-paid.
N.B. The Trade supplied with Boiler Plate and Sheet Iron
every description.

Pontardawe tinplate works, *c*. 1880, with Ynysderw Farm shown alongside. The works was erected by William Parsons in 1835 for the production of boiler plate and tinplate. Note that the 1840 advertisement from *The Cambrian* refers to the Primrose Works, not the Pontardawe Works. The manufactory was constructed alongside the Swansea Canal so that supplies of coal, iron, tin, and finished goods could easily be brought to, and taken from, the works. Two hundred men and boys were employed here in the 1840s and the *Cambrian* advertisement identifies the machinery in use at that time and the type of goods produced.

Pontardawe steelworks, *c*. 1960. The original tinplate works and (later) sheet mills stood where the locomotive is running. The later tinplate works (erected 1911) lies in the distance to the right. On the far left is part of the bar mill and behind, to the right, are the casting pit and melting shop respectively. The long building in the centre foreground was presumably part of the former sheet annealing house. The white building to the right abuts the wagon shop.

Pontardawe steelworks, *c*. 1960. The small building in the foreground is the steelworks manager's office. Far left is part of the power-house of the former tinplate works. To the right of the 140-foot stacks (demolished *c*. 1965) are the melting shop and casting pit on which the Somerfield supermarket now stands.

The steelworks, *c*. 1958, showing from left to right the (former) billet mill, bar mill, casting pit and melting shop. The white-roofed buildings are the tinplate works including the assorting room and boxroom which became the Economic Pressworks about this time. Just below centre is the blacksmith's shop. Also to be seen are the works pond (left), the sewerage (bottom right, built 1901-03), the 'wooden' bridge (centre right) and above it, to the right, the old chemical works. Note the slag tip. It is difficult to believe that the verdant splendour of Ynysderw Farm (117 acres) once covered this site or that Parc Ynysderw does so today.

Pontardawe tinworkers, *c.* 1940. The man sitting front left has a leather pad on his left hand for opening tin plates. Two of the men in the centre are holding spanners and are probably maintenance crew. The remainder are possibly the assorters – men who arranged the tin sheets by size in preparation for packing.

Pontardawe steelworkers, *c.* 1940. Most of the men have a sweat rag around their necks which readily shows how arduous work was in the steel and tinplate industries. The wagon behind has the initials 'WG' painted on its side, a reminder of William Gilbertson and Co., owners of the works until 1933. The wagon contains steel billets and has presumably come from the billet mill.

A group of openers at Pontardawe tinplate works, early this century. The ladies are holding the tin-slasher's knife which was used to force apart tinplates that had become stuck during the hot rolling process. They are not wearing the traditional opener's gloves that contained a lead pad on the palm which would have been used to hit the plates to loosen them. Mrs Elizabeth Rees (*née* Williams) is sitting in the centre row on the left wearing a striped tunic.

Pontardawe tinplate workers from the cleansing department, mid-1950s. The tinplate works was in the ownership of The Steel Company of Wales (founded 1947) at this time and, when it closed in October 1957, the majority of men were offered employment at the new SCOW steelworks at Margam.

The last tapping at the steelworks, September 1962. The ladle is full to capacity and overflowing into the pit alongside. Once the ladles were full of liquid steel they were teemed (poured) into ingot moulds. In the late 1950s and early 1960s the ingots were despatched to Ebbw Vale strip mill for rolling into steel sheet for tinplate.

Last day at the steelworks, 29 September 1962, showing to the right the time office and behind the 'scruff house' and former tinhouse. William Gilbertson and Co. Ltd was acquired by Richard Thomas and Co. Ltd in 1933, though it traded under its old name until 1946 when it was totally absorbed by Richard Thomas and Baldwins Ltd. The tinplate works was acquired by the Steel Company of Wales in May 1947 but the steelworks was retained by RTB. The tinplate works closed in 1957 when 270 were made redundant. The closure of the steelworks in 1962 made 380 redundant and brought to an end some 130 years of tinplate and steel manufacture on the site.

Lucy at the loco shed, 1956. This was a locomotive manufactured by Hudswell's in 1920. Pontardawe steel and tinplate works had a fleet of six steam locomotives: *Lucy*, *Pontardawe*, *James Watt*, *Dorothy*, *Fine Don*, and 'No. 795' – an ex-GWR locomotive manufactured in 1929.

Glanrhyd tinplate works, viewed from Railway Terrace, *c.* 1950. Built in 1879 by the Glantawe Tin Plate Company, the Glantawe tinplate works was acquired by Arthur Gilbertson in 1883 and re-registered as the Glanrhyd Tin Plate Company. It was later sold by W. Gilbertson and Co. in 1901 but reacquired by them in 1928. The five tinplate mills lie behind the furthest stack. To the left of the nearest stack are the annealing, black pickling and cold rolls departments while to the right are the tinhouse and (behind) the assorting room. The works finally closed in 1953 and was subsequently demolished. The 'log works' then occupied the site for a few years. The area today has been designated the Glanrhyd Riverside Park.

Pontardawe (Alloy) sheetworks, 1949. This manufactured blackplate and sheet, the latter sent for galvanising to the Whitford Works, Briton Ferry. In 1918 W. Gilbertson and Co. erected a mill for rolling alloy-steel round bars for making artillery shells. The war ended before the works came into operation. Six sheet mills were built on the Alloy site in 1921. It was known as the New Sheet Works to differentiate it from the old one built in 1899 on the site of the original tinplate works. The long building in the foreground housed the cold rolls, annealing and sheet mills. To the right of the nearest stack are the shear-house and circle cutters and roll grinders establishment.

Demolition of the sheetworks' stacks *c.* 1962. The works temporarily closed on 18 January 1958 and permanently on 15 November 1958, 365 being made redundant. It had operated continuously except for a period during the Second World War. Dismantling of the works commenced in October 1961 and the site was cleared by early 1962. New factories on the Alloy Industrial Estate came in 1965.

Alloy sheetworks mill-team, 1 March 1952, consisting of rollerman, behinder, doubler, and mill-hands posing with a sheet of red-hot steel. Normally, one man would handle a sheet of steel of these dimensions. The photograph shows the screw-down mechanism which was hand operated at this works. The mill-team are, from left to right: Harry Price, William Davy Williams (on 'screw-down'), Sam Jenkins, Ken Jones.

Hot mill and mill-team at the Alloy sheetworks, 1 March 1952. The mill consisted of two upright mill-standards housing a pair of rolls which had pressure exerted through the hand-operated screw-down mechanism. After passing the sheet of steel through the rolls the gears were turned down by the mill-hands using the long handles attached to each gear wheel. The rolls had to be continually adjusted all day long as the sheets were rolled and a new sheet introduced to the mill. Harry Price is standing on the left with the open tongs, and either Sam Jenkins or Ken Jones has his back to us as the rollerman.

Mill-hands at the Alloy sheetworks playing cards due to a breakdown in the works. A mill-roll has broken and the team are waiting for it to be replaced by the maintenance crew. Mill-rolls occasionally fractured if too much pressure was exerted during the rolling process. Harry Price is facing the camera on the left, Bill Barton, centre, is smoking a cigarette. Alongside him is Jim Battenbough and William Davy Williams is on the right with a hand of cards. Gilbertson's offered annual prizes to the rollermen if they did not break a roll throughout a year.

No 2 mill-team at the Alloy sheetworks, 1 March 1952. The whole team can be identified: bar-dragger, furnaceman, labourer, rollerman, behinder, doubler, shearer, marker, foreman. From left to right, front row: Ifan Davies, labourer; Gomer Humphreys, behinder; William Davy Williams, furnaceman. Centre right, with dust coat and flat cap, is Dick Cooper, gaffer (foreman). Back row: Jim Battenbough, bar-dragger; Harry Price, breakerdown; Sam Jenkins, rollerman; Denis Stead, doubler; Gwyn Bowen, shearer; Mr Stead, marker. In the Welsh mills 'shearer' was pronounced 'sharer'.

The former Bryn tinplate works, Ynysmeudwy (centre), *c.* 1965. In operation from 1879 to February 1901, the Ynysmeudwy tinplate works was erected on the site of the former Ynysmeudwy Pottery, both industries being constructed alongside the Swansea Canal because of the benefits of bulk transport to bring in materials and take finished goods to Swansea for sale or export. The Bryn works (registered in September 1901) became part of Richard Thomas and Co. Ltd in 1935. During the Second World War the tinworks machinery was removed as scrap metal to support the war effort in 1941 (the works' last year of operation) and the buildings used as a sugar storage depot by the Ministry of Supply.

Shearers in the Bryn tinplate works, 1920s. The first operation in the tinplate works was that of cutting ('shearing') the 20-foot-long lengths of steel bar, known as 'tin bar' into short lengths required for the furnaces and hot mills. The shearers are using a steam-powered shears. Note the flywheel in the background to maintain the shearing action of the bar cutter, and the stacks of sheared bars between the two men. Langdon Walker is nearest the shears.

Bryn tinplate works, *c*. 1920, showing men in typical mill-workers' uniform of wooden-soled clogs, shirt, apron, and sweat rag. The man only has a short-handled tongs which was used for picking up fairly cold steel sheets. He could possibly be a doubler.

Bryn tinplate works, *c*. 1900. The girls are wearing typical opener's costume of a South Wales tinplate works. Opening tinplates stuck together after the rolling process was a task traditionally carried out by female labour. The girls are wearing canvas aprons to protect their bodies from being cut by the sharp edges of the tinplates. Not so common are the straw boaters worn by two of the openers. The young boy is probably the scrap bundler who gathered up the off-cuts of tinplate after the shearing operation. No doubt the older gentleman is the gaffer.

Five

Coal, Pottery and other Industries

It would be inaccurate to see the evolution of the district purely in terms of tinplate and steel manufacture. Several of the communities had their origins in mining activity, for example: Gellinudd, Rhos and Alltwen. Even when tinplate and steel assumed predominance coal mining was still significant and accounted for 35, 47, 49 and 36 per cent of households in Alltwen, Gellinudd, Rhos and Trebanos respectively in 1891. The principal collieries (with their approximate dates of opening) were Ynisfechan (1813), Waun Coed (1828) Cwmnantllwyd (1830 and 1890), Old Primrose (1840), Cwmnantllici (1873), Cwmnant Du (1880), Daren (1890), New Primrose (1895), Tarenni (1903) and Abernant (1957). There were also numerous smaller drift mines in the district. Other industries to emerge included a chemical works, pottery, brickworks, fire-clay works, foundry, woollen mills, corn and flour mills, gas, quarrying and mineral water manufacture.

The district is, of course, no longer dominated by heavy industry. The tinplate- (1957), sheet- (1958) and steelworks (1962) had all closed by the early 1960s while Abernant, the last of the deep mines, ceased production in 1988. They have been superseded as local employers by light engineering and service industries on the Alloy Industrial Estate (from 1965) and from the late 1950s on (what is now) Parc Ynysderw, itself designated on 12 June 1979. The proposal in April 1955 for a nuclear power station to be sited in the area fortunately never came to fruition.

Rhyd-y-fro corn mill, *c*. 1926, approximately at the time when it fell into disuse. It comprised a large storage room on the ground floor, milling-room over and a two-stall stable. The wheel measured 18 ft by 4½ft. The agricultural community was dependent on the mill which originally formed part of the Nydfwch and the Penllergaer estates. It subsequently came into the ownership of the Revd Josiah Rees but was sold in 1919 by Howel Gwyn Jeffreys to W. Gilbertson & Co., who bought it because it was said to be robbing the works of water from the river. The tenant for many years was Daniel Morgan who also occupied the adjoining Tir Shet or Mill Farm. A heap of debris today, the mill's remains are close to a stone bridge of remarkable architecture built in 1811 by Ben Wallace, a Belgian.

Engine house and timber head-frame carrying winding-sheaves (pulley-wheels) at Primrose Colliery, Rhos, 1920. There were two Primrose collieries working the area around Rhos. The first mine was sunk here by John Parsons in 1840, and a new mine opened in 1895. The colliery 'take' (the area to be worked) extended from Cilybebyll through Bryncoch to Pen-y-Wern overlooking Neath. Glan Llechau House on Primrose Lane, Rhos, was the former offices of the first Primrose Colliery.

Daren Colliery, Trebanos in 1956, showing underground workers helping to repair a coal face at the mine. The Hughes seam was struck in 1880s but there was no major development until c. 1904 when the Graig Colliery Co. was formed. Coal was used locally and also exported via the Swansea Canal but an aerial ropeway was also constructed to convey the coal from the mine over a portion of the village to the railhead at Ynysymond where it was loaded (see p. 67). A branch railway was later constructed as were washing and screening facilities. Pit ponies were also used. Llewellyn Bros. took over ownership in 1932 and some 1,200 tons were mined per week until nationalisation. The colliery closed in 1964.

Tarenni Colliery, Godre'r Graig. This was an anthracite mine opened in 1903 by the South Wales Primrose Coal Co. Ltd (established 1893) to work the Red Vein under Ynys Wil Hernyn Farm land. At various times the company also owned Cwmnantllwyd mine and Waun Coed Colliery. The 320 workers at Tarenni Colliery were given notice to quit by the NCB (National Coal Board) on 5 November 1948 and the mine closed down immediately.

COLLIERY FLOODED IN THE SWANSEA VALLEY.

General view of the Tarni Colliery, in the Swansea Valley. While 227 miners were at work below an alarming inrush of water occurred, and four men were drowned outright. Great pluck was shown by the various members of the rescue parties. ("Daily Mirror" photograph.)

Mr. Rees. Mr Cloe. Mr. Jones. Mr. Williams. Mr. Davis.

Mr. Hopkin Rees, the under-manager, and Mr. Sam Jones, the overman, proceeded through the workings with remarkable coolness directly the inrush of water occurred, and pointed out to the men the means of escaping. Mr. Cloe, the assistant master at Godregraig School, even stripped the shirt from his back to give to one of the escaped men, who had come up almost unclad. Messrs. Norris Williams and Evan Davis performed excellent work with the rescue parties.—("Daily Mirror" photographs.)

A B C D E

Members of a rescue party—(A) Mr. D. Rees, (B) Mr. J. Thomas, (C) Mr. D. Williams, (D) Mr. J. Harris, (E) Mr. G. Lewis.—("Daily Mirror" photograph.)

Tarenni pit disaster, 1 November 1909. This was one of the most calamitous colliery floodings ever experienced in the Swansea Valley. Water from the disused Ynysgeinon Pit broke into Tarenni at 1.30 p.m. on Monday afternoon at the top stall of No 6 heading. 230 men and boys were underground at the time of the inrush of water, five of whom were to lose their lives. Many colliers were rescued by workmates who pulled men to safety out of the torrent. Those who lost their lives were David Edward Rees, Ystalyfera (aged 18); Ben Griffiths, Ystalyfera (19); Evan Thomas, Gellinudd (19); Evan Harries, Alltwen (19) and Isaac Rees, Ynysmeudwy (36).

Unveiling ceremony by the general manager of No 9 area, Mr G.A. Watson, and the cutting of the first sod at Abernant Colliery, Pontardawe, 7 January 1954. This new NCB pit was estimated to cost £7 million and produce 3,000 tons of coal daily with a workforce of 2,000 people. Amongst those present were: Mr D.N. Simpson, Abernant, chief planning engineer; G.W. Strong, site engineer; Daniel Thomas, divisional electrical engineer; T.L. Price, transmission and power supply engineer; S.T. Richards, area electrical engineer; Daniel Jones, area production department; H.C. Bisp, area production engineer; Roger Griffiths, area mechanical engineer; D.R. Williams, contractor; G.M. Harris, man-power and welfare officer; W.T. Rees, area labour officer; Evan Lewis, area administrative officer; A.W. Lavington, area chief accountant; W.E. Lea Thomas, area chief surveyor; R.G. Morris, coal preparation manager; Bryn Thomas, area supplies officer; Iorwerth Morgan, group surveyor; Vincent Richards, chief clerk production department; John Hopkins, area consultative secretary.

Bottom of the shaft at Abernant Colliery, 6 March 1958, with pit sinkers employed by Thyssens Ltd extending the workings out from pit-bottom. A number of accidents occurred while sinking the colliery, including two fatalities. Irishman, Martin Brennan was killed on 23 September 1954, and another pit-sinker, Matyas Petrokovis, an Hungarian, was killed when he fell 750 feet down the shaft in December 1961.

Extending the underground roadways at Abernant Colliery, 6 March 1958. Note the ventilation system on the right to provide fresh air for the pit sinkers, and also the water jug. The rock faces on the heading sides and roof have been drilled and bolts inserted to support the wire mesh preventing falls of stone.

The chemical works, viewed *c.* 1925 from the railway station. This three-acre establishment incorporating part of Pontardawe Mill lands was founded *c.* 1849 by Jacob Lewis, a Swansea draper. It supplied the tinplate industry in the district primarily with vitriol or sulphuric acid (used in the pickling process) and initially would have had access to the wider community via the private Primrose Canal. Jacob Lewis lived at Ynysygelynen House. His son, Lewis, lived at 'Brynheulog' and was also involved in the concern, as was his son Sidney. The works was in severe decline by the early 1940s, though the site was subsequently used by Russell Davies, haulage contractor. Many will recall the 'Pompeiian' remains of 'The Chemy' before the site was cleared in the 1970s.

Ynysmeudwy Pottery workers, 1871. The Ynysmeudwy factory produced fire-bricks, chimney tops, terra-cotta ware, drain pipes, and earthenware (china). The gentleman, front left, is holding a trowel in each hand and is presumably a moulder employed to produce the various moulds required for making bricks, decorative tiles, jugs and vases. It has been suggested he is Thomas Vaughan, the foreman at the factory in 1871.

Ynysmeudwy vase, 1856. This was a commemorative piece produced to celebrate the state visit of Napoleon III, Emperor of France (1852-70), to Britain in April 1856. The floral design around the rim of the jug is the Ynysmeudwy 'Alma' pattern.

Pontardawe Brewery, which was completed in 1838 by John Jones of Ynysderw Farm ('Shôn Ynysderw') replacing an older brewery nearby. It was constructed on the canal-side to enable boats to carry barrels of beer to the public houses along the route of the canal. Ownership passed to Robert Evans between 1848 and 1859 and later the brewery became part of the David Evans brewery empire from 1871 to 1946. The chimney stacks for the steam machinery are visible in this photograph.

Blacksmith's shop *c.* 1930. This traditional blacksmith's shop was on the bank of the canal. The brewery can be seen in the background. One of the smiths at work is Fred Suff.

PONTARDAWE, SWANSEA VALLEY.

Sale of Capital Iron Foundry Premises, Plant, Machinery, &c.

Mr. WILLIAM HARRY REES
Has received instructions
TO SELL BY AUCTION,
At the Premises, on FRIDAY, SEPTEMBER 29, 1871 (unless previously disposed of by Private Contract),

ALL that Capital IRON FOUNDRY and Fitting Shop known as the "Canal Side Foundry," with the premises thereto belonging, containing in the whole One Acre, or thereabouts, situate close to Ynisgelynen, Pontardawe, now or lately in the occupation of Messrs. Howell and Stephen: together with the whole of the MACHINERY, PLANT, FITTINGS, &c., &c., therein, including an 8-inch vertical engine, 2ft. stroke, complete; tube boiler, 12ft. by 4ft. 6in., nearly new; blacking mill, standards and pulley, head gearing. a 12in. centre screw cutting late, 15ft. bed, in good condition; vice and bench, tool chest and tools, drilling gear and John Bull, sundries in fitting shop, Pulley belts, a 2ft. 8in. blowing fan and pulley, iron cupola, 12ft. by 3ft. 9in.; moulders' iron boxes, wooden crane, crabb and blocks, wrought iron door or stove, sundry cast iron, sundry wrought iron, wooden patterns for engines, wooden patterns for water wheels, blacksmiths' bellows, anvil, strong punching machine, egg-end boiler, 10ft. by 2ft. 6in., forcer, casting, and sundry other articles too numerous to mention.

The property is held under a Lease granted by Herbert Lloyd, Esq., for a term of 99 years, from March, 1867, subject to the low annual ground rent of £6.

The premises are conveniently situated with a frontage to the Swansea canal, and good road approaches, and possess facilities for doing a greatly increased trade.

The Foundry Premises will be offered for sale at half-past one, and the sale of Plant and Machinery will commence at two o'clock.

For further particulars apply to Mr. James Kempthorne, Solicitor, Neath; to Mr. D. Smith, Estate Agent, Alltwen, Pontardawe; to Messrs. Jones and Howell, Railway Bridge Works, Neath; and to the Auctioneer, Neath.

Auction and Printing Offices, Neath,
September, 1871.

Pontardawe foundry and fitting shop. The foundry was established in 1865 by Thomas Howells and Thomas Stevens and was later owned (1871) by T. Howells and J. Howells. The foundry was closed from 1919 to 1930 before being re-opened by Wilfred H. Morgan and Wilfred S. Evans as the Pontardawe Foundry and Engineering Company Ltd. The furnace stack was raised in 1995 to comply with current emission standards.

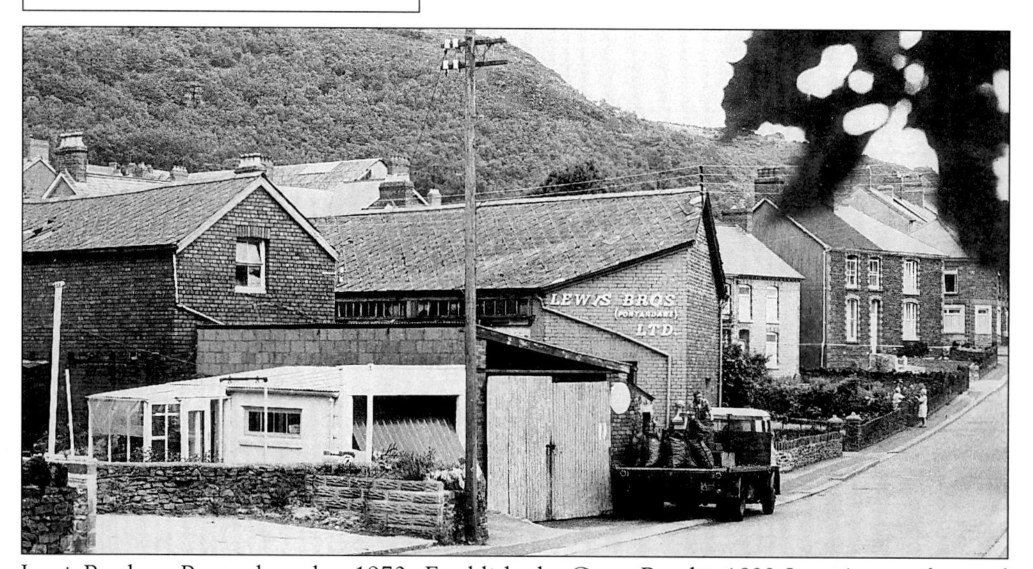

Lewis Brothers, Pontardawe, late 1970s. Established at Grove Road in 1899, Lewis's manufactured mineral waters, squashes, cordials, soda water, ginger beer, vinegar, and sacramental wine. The business also consisted of charabanc hire, coal merchants, and owned the 'Rink' roller-skating and ballroom dancing hall on Works Lane. The title of the business changed to Cwmtawe Minerals in the late 1950s. Mineral water 'pop' production ceased in the mid-1960s and coal deliveries in the 1980s. Amongst those working there in the late 1950s were Mr Arthur Lewis, works manager; Moy Lewis, accounts and administration manager; Dick Ingram, coal deliveries; Jeff Thomas, driver; Bill Thomas, general hand; Elsie Thomas, syrup mixer; Gwladys Key, machine operator; Marjory Thomas, labelling machine; and Philip Pugh, roundsman. The buildings were demolished in October 1990 and a private dwelling erected on the site in 1996.

Six

Gilbertsons and Lloyds

The Gilbertsons exerted a predominant influence in the district in the ninety years they lived there. In that time (1860-1950) the area was transformed from a discrete collection of villages to a thriving urban community. Other landowners played their part in this transition, notably Herbert Lloyd of Plâs Cilybebyll and Howel Gwyn of Neath and Dyffryn Clydach, but it was the Gilbertsons who proved to be the catalysts for fundamental, irreversible change. Although not of 'ancient' gentry stock they were nonetheless considered leaders of the community. As upwardly-mobile industrialists, their influence transcended industry and encapsulated the social, religious, philanthropic, educational, musical and sporting spheres.

Unlike the Gilbertsons, the wealth of the Lloyds was primarily rooted in land. They were indirectly descended from the Herberts of Plâs Cilybebyll who were resident there from the late sixteenth century. The Plâs first came into the possession of the Lloyds in 1797 although a lack of direct male heirs caused the surname to disappear from 1817 to 1849 when it was reassumed by Francis Edwardes Leach. The Lloyds were also perceived as community leaders and, like the Moore-Gwyns, they intermarried with the Gilbertsons.

William Gilbertson (1810-82), from a portrait painted in 1850. His father Mathias (1777-1870) of Elm Lodge, Egham, Surrey was the second son of James Gilbertson (d. 1826), land agent of the Marquess of Tweeddale. In 1835, Mathias married Fanny Collings, daughter of the King's Messenger, Robert Collings of London.

William Gilbertson, 1873. Trained in the law, he came to Cwmavon in 1839 on being appointed receiver and manager of the Copper Miners Tinplate Co. Ltd. His initial appointment came to an end in 1844 but in 1852 he was reappointed and remained in charge until 1860. Having clearly relished the challenge of running a tinplate works during his period at Cwmavon, he abandoned his career in the law and purchased the tinplate works at Pontardawe and Trebanos from William Parsons, together with Ynysderw House, where he had come to live by 1861. He became a JP, a member of the Pontardawe Board of Guardians and of the Rhyndwyclydach School Board. He was an ardent churchman and a faithful member of St Peter's church where he and his wife, Eliza, are buried.

Eliza Gilbertson (1816-68), *c*. 1860. Born Eliza Bramah, she was the daughter of Francis Bramah of London and granddaughter of Joseph Bramah (1749-1814), the famous inventor. She bore William nine children: Mathias, Francis, Arthur, Edward, Kate, Fanny, Ellen, Madelaine and Maude.

Ynysderw House, April 1985. Built by William Parsons in the 1850s on Ynysderw Farm land, it had come into the ownership of William Gilbertson by 1861. The solicitor, David B. Turberville, and his family were resident in 1891. In 1911 it was home for the curates of All Saints church. On 5 July 1948 it was formally opened as the public health department of Rhyndwyclydach District Council and remained so until 1974. It later became derelict and was demolished in April 1987. A sheltered accommodation complex, which retains the name, is on the site today.

Arthur Gilbertson, *c.* 1850. Born in Cwmavon in 1841, he lived temporarily at Danygraig House but, following his marriage to Ellen Lloyd of Plâs Cilybebyll in 1872, he had a new mansion built at Glanrhyd (*c.* 1879). He was responsible for establishing the '1874 list' which became the basis of all South Wales tinplate workers' wages and in 1877 he was elected President of the South Wales Tinplate Manufacturers Association. He took over full control of the Pontardawe tinplate works in 1882 and in 1883 purchased the Glantawe tinplate works. He built the steelworks at Pontardawe in 1890 and in the same year established the Glynbeudy tinplate works at Brynamman. In his industrial career, Arthur Gilbertson was a pioneer of the Basic Steel process and galvanised sheet. In 1892, he was elected High Sheriff of Glamorgan.

Arthur Gilbertson as High Sheriff, 1892. Arthur was a law unto himself and negotiations with the trade unions were often difficult. He was, however, benevolent and paternal in relation to his workforce providing a reading room, billiard room and recreational ground. He was also deeply religious and a strict sabbatarian. A keen horticulturist and a great student of music, he was considered to be one of the best organists in Wales. He suffered a stroke in 1907 and was an invalid for five years before dying of pneumonia in 1912. He was buried at All Saints church joining his wife and three of his children. In its obituary, *The Cambrian*, considered him 'the virtual founder of the community of Pontardawe'.

Ellen Gilbertson, *c.* 1890. Born Ellen Lloyd in 1850, she was the second daughter of Francis Edwardes Lloyd of Plâs Cilybebyll. She had three brothers: Herbert, Francis Elliot and Richard Carre and one sister, Mary. She married Arthur Gilbertson in 1872 and they had seven sons and seven daughters: Colin; Francis William; Arthur Howell; Cecil; Harriet; Lettice Mary; Olive; Winifred; Charles Geoffrey; Marguerite Ellen; George Noel; Sylvia; Phyllis and John. She died in 1894.

Glanrhyd House, seen in use as an auxiliary hospital, 1917. Built by Arthur Gilbertson (1877-79) on what historically had been Glynmeirch Farm land, it was commandeered for use as an auxiliary hospital for part of the First World War. It was subsequently converted into flats, seventeen people being resident there in 1925. It continued as flats until 1965 when thirteen were resident. The house went into severe decline soon after and was demolished late 1968. The adjacent plantation is now severely overgrown but there are plans to create a country park on the site.

Glanrhyd tennis court, 1904. The Gilbertsons, particularly Charles, were active tennis players (see p. 123). The plantation also included a swimming pool and ornamental ponds (and in later years) the Glanrhyd Nurseries and Gardens.

The Gilbertsons at Glanrhyd 1895. From left to right, standing: Colin (b. 1872); Frank (b. 1873); Arthur (b. 1841); Cecil (b. 1876); Howell (b. 1874). Seated, middle row: Margaret (b. 1885); Harriet (b. 1878); Olive (b. 1881). Seated, front: George Noel (b. 1886); Phyllis (b. 1890); Sylvia (b. 1888); Charles (b. 1884) and Winifred (b. 1883).

Three Gilbertson brothers; from left to right: Cecil, Frank and Charles. They, along with Howell and Colin, succeeded their father in the management of the Pontardawe works. Francis William became chairman, with Cecil and (later) Charles, as co-directors. 'Mr Frank', as Francis was known (1873-1929) lived at 'Glynteg' which he built (1890) on the north side of the ravine of the Upper Clydach River, opposite 'Glanrhyd'. He had an illustrious career being a county councillor, President of the Swansea Metal Exchange, Chairman of the South Wales Siemens Steel Association and first President of the University College of Swansea. 'Mr Cecil' (1876-1948) lived at Abercrave. An excellent athlete he became secretary of the Swansea and Brecon Diocesan Board of Finance and succeeded Frank as chairman of the company.

Charles Gilbertson, c. 1910. On the death of his brother, Colin, he joined his two brothers, Frank and Cecil, in the family business. Born at 'Glanrhyd' in 1884, he married Ellen Moore-Gwyn of Dyffryn Clydach in 1908 and came to live at Gellygron House where they remained until 1950 leaving for 'Broadlands', Laleston that year. They had seven children (Nancy, Joan, Arthur, John, James, David and Geoffrey). He was a man of deep Christian conviction and was active in the work of the church being a member of the governing body of the Church in Wales. He was also a magistrate and member of Glamorgan County Council. His recreational activities included cricket, tennis, athletics and angling and he was the first President of Pontardawe Golf Club, when it was formed in 1924. He died at Laleston in January 1963.

Ellen Christobel Gilbertson, c. 1920. Born Ellen Moore-Gwyn in 1883, the daughter of Joseph Moore-Gwyn, nephew and heir of Howel Gwyn. Her brothers, Gwyn and Howell, also married Gilbertsons (Olive and Winifred, respectively) as did her sister, Gwladys, who married Cecil Gilbertson. In her earlier years Ellen was actively involved with the Girl Guide movement, the Red Cross and during the First World War played a prominent part at Glanrhyd House when it was converted to a hospital for wounded soldiers. She also took a particularly keen and active interest in All Saints church and was president of the ladies guild. Ellen died in December 1963 and like her husband, Charles, is buried at All Saints church.

Gellygron House in 1950. This was the home of Charles and Ellen Gilbertson from 1908, having been acquired from Howel Gwyn Jeffries. The estate was ninety-two acres in 1838 when it was owned by Josiah Rees. In 1851 and 1861, John Morgan, owner of the Waun Coed Colliery, occupied the property. Much earlier, and along with Alltycham, Cefn Llan Isaf and Glynmeirch, Gellygron had formed part of the Nydfwch estate (centred on modern day Cadle) which itself became incorporated into the Penllergaer estate in 1750. Gellygron House became a home for the aged in May 1956.

Interior of Gellygron House, *c.* 1918, showing the drawing room with its organ installed by Charles, who like his father, was an enthusiastic organist.

Swansea Valley bride to be. Presentation by farmers of the district of a silver salver to Miss Joan Gilbertson, daughter of Charles and Ellen, on her marriage, Gellygron House, 13 July 1936. From left to right: D. Morgan; Jenkin Davies (Penygraig); L.B. Williams; Joan Gilbertson; Ellen Gilbertson; Arthur Gilbertson (brother); Charles Gilbertson; Captain A.H. Penderel (Garth); -?-. The wedding of Joan to George Tennant Bruce of Craigie Barns, Dundee, took place at All Saints church on 18 July 1936 the bride wearing ivory satin royale. Some 400 guests were at the church and reception at 'Gellygron'. Over 340 presents were given to the bride and groom.

Charles Gilbertson and family, Gellygron House, Christmas 1939. From left to right, standing: Arthur, John (killed in action in 1944) and his wife Eileen, James, Nancy, David, George Tennant Bruce; seated: Hilarie, Ellen (holding her granddaughter, Phebe), Charles (holding his grandson, Anthony Bruce) and Joan. On the ground, seated: Geoffrey.

William Herbert of Plâs Cilybebyll. The Herberts of Plâs Cilybebyll were descended from Sir George Herbert of The Plâs, Swansea (d. 1570) and were resident at Plâs Cilybebyll from the late sixteenth century. William (d. 1689) was the son of George Herbert and, in 1711, his son Richard (d. 1728) married Elizabeth Lloyd (d. 1771), the daughter of Edward Lloyd of Cilymaenllwyd, Carmarthenshire. She was succeeded by her daughter, Elizabeth, who married Richard Turberville of Ewenny. The house subsequently passed to her kinsman, John Herbert Lloyd in 1797 and successively to his sister, Mrs Jane Bassett, in 1817, and on her death in 1828 to her cousin, Mary Brand Jones of Brawdy, the wife of Henry Leach.

Henry Leach (1770-1848). A colourful and energetic figure of Pembrokeshire mercantile stock, he was appointed as a magistrate in 1801 and Collector of Customs at Milford in 1806. Like John Herbert Lloyd (1753-1817), he proved to be an enterprising manager and 'spirited improver' of the Cilybebyll estate, the house being radically altered during his time. He was elected a Fellow of the Geological Society in 1833 and retired as Collector of Customs in 1842. A staunch Whig in politics he died at Milford in 1848 and was buried at St Thomas' church, Haverfordwest where there is a memorial tablet to his memory.

Plâs Cilybebyll. The origins of the Cilybebyll estate go back to the late fourteenth century, the first identifiable person in the Cilybebyll deeds being John ap Lewis ap Henri in 1507. The property passed to his son, Griffith, and grandson, Lewis, and to Lewis's daughter, Janet, who married George Herbert, son of Matthew Herbert of Swansea. In 1838, the estate was the largest in the district (2,100 acres) comprising sixteen farms. After Henry Leach, the estate passed to his son, Francis Edwardes, who assumed the surname Lloyd as a condition of Jane Bassett's will. It then descended through the generations to Herbert Lloyd (d. 1914) and to John Herbert Purdon Lloyd (d. 1957). It was sold in that year.

Plâs Cilybebyll Lodge, *c.* 1910. Together with the adjoining garden, it measured one rood and ten perches in 1838 (a rood being a quarter-acre and 40 perches = 1 rood). The thatched edifice was built to resemble the shape of a kraal and survived until the early 1960s when it was destroyed by fire. It has since been thoroughly modernised. In 1891, Jacob Beach, a 53-year-old gamekeeper lived here with his wife and two daughters.

Herbert and Frances Lloyd, *c.* 1870. Herbert (1838-1914) was the eldest son of Francis Edwardes Lloyd (1805-65). He was educated at Marlborough Grammar School, Rugby and Cambridge. He studied land agency at Castle Troy, County Limerick where he met Frances Hariette Purdon (1838-1929) of Tinerana, County Clare, who he married in 1864. He was JP for Glamorgan and Breconshire, High Sheriff of Glamorgan (1877), chairman of the Pontardawe Board of Guardians (1878-1909) and of the Pontardawe Rural District Council (1894-5, 1900-1, 1902-3, 1903-4). A keen sportsman and a good shot, he devoted much time to farming and 'believed in working alongside his servants'. He is buried at Cilybebyll church. Frances was the eldest daughter of Simon George Purdon (d. 1862) and his wife Louisa Elizabeth Eleanor, daughter of the Rt Revd Richard Ponsonby, Bishop of Derry and Raphoe.

Herbert Lloyd, with four of his daughters, making hay at Cilybebyll, *c.* 1900. Herbert and Frances had eleven children: Louisa Henrietta, Ada, Gertrude, John Herbert Purdon, Ethel, Counceletta, Nina Augusta, Richard Godfrey William, Norah, Harry Ponsonby and Lionel Robert. Six daughters and John were recorded on the 1891 census along with a cook, parlourmaid, two housemaids, a kitchenmaid, two dairywomen and a groom.

Seven

Streets

The tithe map (p. 8) shows the basic highway infrastructure of Pontardawe in 1838 comprising what later became known as Herbert Street, High Street, James Street, Alltycham Drive, Dynevor Terrace and Glanrhyd Road. The main road to Swansea from The Cross (or Pont Clydach) however followed the present Works Lane. There were no named streets in the 1851 census but by 1861, five had appeared: Neath Road (the forerunner of Herbert Street); Ynysygelynen Row; Maes Iago; Primrose Row and Swansea Road. Between 1871 and 1881 names were applied to High Street, James Street, Herbert Street, Holly Street, Orchard Street, George Street, Thomas Street and Brecon Road. Arthur Street, Court Lane and Prospect Place had appeared by 1891. By 1898 Grove Road, Church Street and Derw Road had been built as had part of Ynisderw Road while Francis Street was in embryo. Woodfield Road (Coedcae) was built in 1903 and Woodfield Road from 1905. Others appearing before 1918 were Smithfield (1905-06) Birchfield Road (1906), Heathfield (1908) and Western Road, Uplands Road, Tawe Terrace, Quarr Road, Jones Street and Hopkin Street. The process was continued in the 1930s with the building of Bronywawr, (most of) Brynawel, Alltywerin and Gwyrddgoed and from 1947 by the rest of Brynawel, Ffordd Silkin, and West Crossways.

In Alltwen the earliest named streets (1861) were Mill Row, Banwen, Queen Street (later Gwyn Street), Orchard Row and Incline Dramroad. By 1881, Gwyn Street, Alltwen Hill, Graig Road, Dyffryn Road, Edward Street, Railway Terrace and Brondeg Lane are named or were in existence. In Trebanos the earliest (1861) were Swansea Road, Daren Road and Glynmeirch Road and by 1891 nine other thoroughfares had appeared, principally on Graig Trebanos. In Ynysmeudwy, the earliest phase of named streets occurred between 1871 and 1881, when in addition to Ynysmeudwy Row (pre-1871), Ynysmeudwy Road, Gellyfowy Road, Craig Llangiwg Road and Craig Ynysmeudwy Road had appeared.

Alltwen Hill, *c.* 1910. A pre-1799 thoroughfare. To the right is Mill Row built in the 1850s on Pontardawe (Flour) Mill land. There were six households recorded here in 1891, headed by a doubler, brander, tin boxer and blackplate assorter, tinman and two labourers. The Hill had a population of 373 in 1891 and comprised 80 households, 19 of which were associated with the tinplate trade and 16 with the coal mines.

Two views of Rhos. The earlier one above dates from *c.* 1900. These parts of the village are instantly recognisable today. The house to the centre left (above), Ty Mawr, became the Rhos branch of the Alltwen and Pontardawe Co-operative Society Ltd about this time. It is shown (below, right) *c.* 1920. Rhos village numbered 220 in 1891 with another eighty living in the immediate district. It would increase again following the opening of the New Primrose Colliery, built in 1895 on Forest Goch land. Below, in the distance, is Ebenezer Independent Chapel built on Cefn Celfi land and incorporated in 1896.

Rhyd-y-fro, *c.* 1900, with an early view of Commercial Road. The properties on the right are pre-1838 and still survive though much modernised. The Royal Oak can be seen in the background. In 1891, Sarah Phillips, a 45-year-old widow was head of the household with her two sons, one daughter and a boarder. This too is of pre-1838 origin. Rhyd-y-fro village in 1891 contained some 190 inhabitants.

Swansea Road, Trebanos, *c.* 1910. The house on the left is 153 Swansea Road. Note in the distance the disused aerial ropeway for the Daren Colliery which transported coal across the valley to the Midland Railway until the Great Western Railway completed the Clydach to Cwmgors branch line as far as Trebanos in 1915. The ropeway was built in 1899 but caused many legal disputes, for example, damaged chimneys. The Daren closed in 1964.

Curtis Row (now Ynysmeudwy Road), Ynysmeudwy *c.* 1910. Erected by the Ynysmeudwy Pottery Company in 1853 to house its workers, these houses were originally named Ynysmeudwy Row, but known locally as 'The Barracks'. The factory was started by the brothers, Michael and William Williams in 1845. Michael Williams's daughter, Elizabeth, married a Bristol accountant, John Curtis, in 1849. She became heiress to the Ynysmeudwy estate and her descendants owned the houses until the early years of the twentieth century, hence the naming of the houses as Curtis Row.

Upper Ynysmeudwy village in 1911. The upper village developed around Ynysmeudwy Pottery and Ynysmeudwy Uchaf Farm after the pottery company began erecting workers' dwellings in 1848 with a second phase of building from 1853. The houses to the right are the first dwellings in the new village, constructed in 1848. The old Cwm-Du river bridge is in the foreground and the cow byre of Ynysmeudwy Uchaf Farm (white building), which was seriously damaged by fire in 1958, is in the background.

Road widening, James Street, October 1936. Top: looking towards Pontardawe, with 62 James Street on the extreme right. On the left is the entrance to 'Brynheulog' with the Lewis' car in view. Below: looking towards Gellygron. On the top left is 'Glynteg' built by F.W. Gilbertson in 1890. It is a private nursing home today. James Street, incorporating Maes Iago, had a population of 275 in 1891, a third of its forty-nine heads of household working in the tinplate works. There were also three wool weavers, the Maes Iago woollen factory being the main establishment (pre-1860).

Pontardawe High Street, *c*. 1910. Prominent on the left is the ironmonger's shop of Davies & Company, erected in 1854 and opened in 1855. On the right is the 'Ale and Porter' stores, now 'The Café on the Square'. The Alltwen and Pontardawe co-operative building, erected in 1890, is the tall building on the right.

A superb view of old Pontardawe showing The Cross, 1909. Davies the ironmonger's has hardly changed but The Cross Hotel was then still a small establishment with its cast-iron entrance porch. Robert Evans, aged 47, was recorded as the inn-keeper in the 1881 census. The roads are mostly unmade and consist of crushed stone. Modern vehicles are evident with the car opposite the co-operative buildings and the bicycle outside Davies the ironmonger's. Electric street lighting only appears on the approach to the bridge. At that time, surplus electricity was supplied from the steelworks to a limited number of locations in the town; at night-time the rest of the town was in darkness. Note the lady on the right nursing a child in a shawl 'Welsh fashion'.

Herbert Street from The Cross in 1905 a time when horse-drawn traffic 'ruled OK!' It was named after Herbert Lloyd of Plâs Cilybebyll. Part of the two-storey Cross Hotel is to the left. Plans to enlarge the hotel to its present size were submitted in 1908. Note the gradient ahead towards the humped-back canal bridge. The furthest property on the left was London House, drapers. Herbert Street had a population of 361 in 1891. Of the sixty-seven households over a third were involved with the tinplate trade.

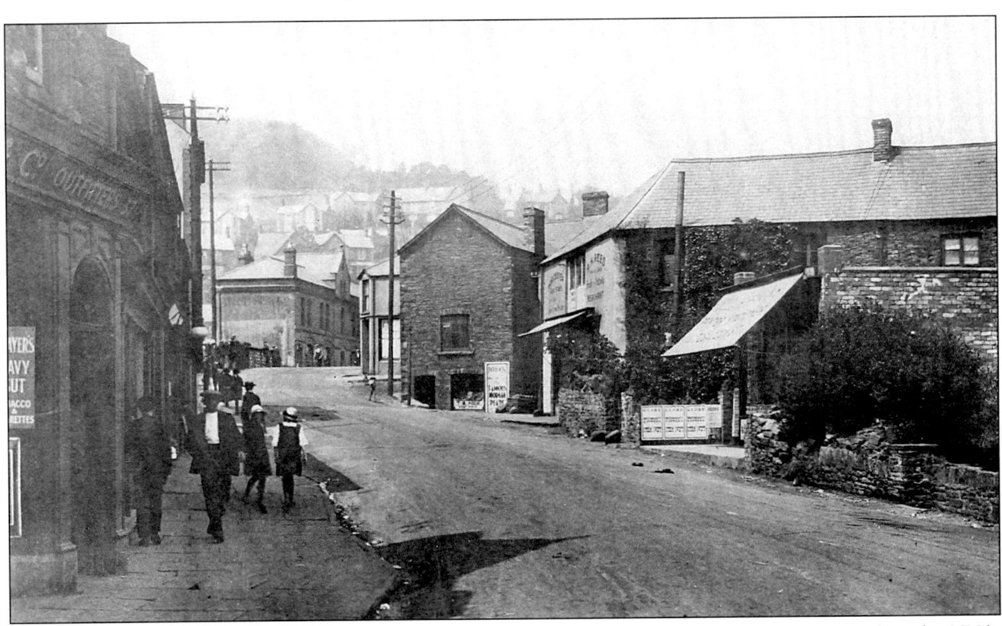

Herbert Street in the 1940s showing, near right, the *West Wales Observer* office (closed 1978). Beyond is R.H. Rees, fruit and potato merchant. To the left is William Davies & Co., general drapers, tailors, outfitters, milliners and hatters, formerly C.R. & W. Davies and part of the Victoria Buildings erected in 1887.

Lower Herbert Street, *c.* 1905, showing along the right the boundary wall of Ynysygelynen House. The properties on the left are today, from left to right: Kwik Silver and Elcee's café; A&M Taxis and Minibus Hire; Toque Fashions; Tudor T. Evans (family butcher); Village Shoe Shop; Indian Cottage & Tandoori Restaurant; vacant (formerly the pharmacy); A. & A. Taylor (newsagent); Southern Fried Chicken; vacant (formerly G.R. & W. Morgan family butcher).

Floods, lower Herbert Street, 1912. Up until recent times when remedial measures were put in place, it was common for the Upper Clydach River to burst its banks with devastating consequences for households. Note the building which became the Jubilee Club in 1935. The houses on the right and immediate left are of pre-1875 origin.

High Street, Pontardawe, *c.* 1915, with the road consisting of crushed stone and pavements only on one side. A stream flows down the street on the left-hand side. Only one motor vehicle is present, at the junction of Thomas Street and High Street. The building between the two telegraph posts on the left is the police station. High Street had a population of 286 in 1891. Of the fifty-five households, a third were associated with the tinplate trade. Other occupations included grocers (4), coal miners (3), blacksmiths (3), publicans (2), a brewer and an inspector of police.

The Avenue, *c.* 1910. Only the rump of what was The Avenue survives today. To the left, are the grounds of Ynysderw House and to the right the field where the works pond was situated. All of this was once Ynysderw Farm land.

Thomas Street, 1930. A pre-1875 highway built on Tir y Bont land (Cae'r Derwen and Waun Isaf), owned by the Cilybebyll estate. In 1891, 184 people lived there in thirty-four households, fourteen of whose heads worked in the tinplate trade. Other occupations included three carpenters and two brewery workers. Note Tabernacle and the police station (top).

Alltycham, Bronywawr, showing the houses under construction in the early 1930s. The houses were built in the 'garden village' style with gardens at front and rear, stylish gables to the roofs, porches over the front doors, and adequate space between properties.

Eight

Buildings and Shops

The coming of industry saw the development of urbanisation and commercial expansion resulting in dramatic and irreversible topographical change. The most visible manifestations were churches and chapels whose erection was often the result of beneficence on the part of industrialists and landowners. Altruism went only so far, however, and they saw to it that their opulent lifestyles were secured by the building of genteel mansions for themselves. Principal among these were 'Ynysderw', 'Danygraig', 'Glanrhyd', 'Glynteg', 'Brynheulog' and 'Ynysmeudwy' while others such as 'Gellygron' and 'Alltycham' were refined and upgraded. Pontardawe itself became the centre of civic government for the district of Rhyndwyclydach in 1894, having already been the administrative head of a Poor Law Union since 1875.

Signs of modernism and maturity were also apparent in other urban spheres. For example among places of entertainment were reading rooms, dance halls, skating rinks, concert halls and (in later years) theatres and cinemas. Public houses and hotels were also much in evidence. In 1891 they numbered ten in Pontardawe, two in Rhyd-y-fro, two in Ynysmeudwy, two in Trebanos, one in Rhos, one in Gellinudd and eight in Alltwen. A police station had been built in 1867 while other buildings to appear were post offices, a telephone exchange, banks and a fire station. But it was the Public Hall and Institute, opened in 1909, which perhaps best reflected the growing confidence of the community. The main commercial artery of Pontardawe has always been Herbert Street. All manner of shops and retail premises were here at the turn of the century – drapers, milliners, ironmongers, grocers, tailors, boot and shoemakers, confectioners, butchers etc. In Trebanos, commerce has centred on Swansea Road while in Alltwen it has been the linear thoroughfare of Alltwen Hill.

48 Brecon Road, Pontardawe, c. 1920. This was originally a small holding called Halfway (later Tir-y-bont) and was part of the Cilybebyll estate. In 1838, this row of cottages were amongst the very few buildings along present-day Brecon Road. A stone stairway was built into the chimney-breast of the pine end wall. From the late 1950s to 1980s one of the cottages operated as a butcher's shop under the patronage of 'Des the Butcher'.

Pontardawe police station on High Street. Taken post-1919, this photograph shows several of the policemen wearing military campaign ribbons from the First World War. In the central doorway are the inspector and sergeant and on each side three constables. Note the curtains in the left-hand window which was the portion of the building occupied by the station inspector and his family.

RDC offices. The Pontardawe Rural District Council had, like its predecessor the Pontardawe Rural Sanitary Authority, previously met in the Poor Law Union workhouse (later the Danybryn Hostel), the first meeting being held on 28 December 1894 under the chairmanship of Herbert Lloyd. The new office (later extended, left) was opened *c*. 1907, the premises being known as the Union Office as it also held the meetings of the Pontardawe Poor Law Union Board of Guardians whose last meeting in the workhouse was 11 April 1907. The RDC and, from 1974 its successor Lliw Valley Borough Council, were occupants until 1979. The building subsequently became the magistrates court. The Public Hall lies ahead.

Pontardawe Workhouse c. 1920. This evocative picture shows the stark nature of the building which was constructed in 1879 four years after the formation of the Pontardawe Poor Law Union. It cost £8,890 to hold 130 inmates. The first meeting of the Board of Guardians was on 14 April 1875. Among the guardians present were J.P. Budd, W. Gilbertson, H. Lloyd and H.N. Miers. In 1891, the institution held twenty-two inmates (including seven children), the workhouse master being Robert Short. Also shown is Ynysmeudwy Isaf (centre left) and bottom left, the Glantawe Bridge, where it crossed 'The Cinders'. Built in c. 1879 to connect with the Glantawe tinplate works, it was washed away in 1933.

The Local Government Act of 1929 transferred the responsibilities of the Poor Law guardians to Glamorgan County Council. The workhouse was renamed a 'public assistance institution' and remained so until 1948. It subsequently became the Danybryn Hostel (seen here). This closed in August 1988 and was subsequently demolished. Sheltered accommodation stands on the site today.

'Welcome to the Queen of Song'. The day Adelina Patti opened the Public Hall and Institute, 6 May 1909. Taken on the canal bridge, Herbert Street.

Herbert Street, on the day the Public Hall opened in May 1909. The men shown here were the 'Arches Committee' and comprised, from left to right: Evan Morgan, Phil Hopkin, William Williams, Johnny Roberts (Vine Villa), Evan Hopkin, Tom Lewis and Ben Lewis. The large house to the right (Laurel Cottage) was demolished in the early 1960s. One of the two white houses behind is said to be where Ben Davies, the internationally renowned opera singer, lived for a short time. Both were demolished in the mid- to late 1970s. The car park now stands on this site which was historically Cae Pandy, part of Ynysygelynen Farm.

The Public Hall and Institute, *c.* 1914. Built on Ynysygelynen land owned by the Cilybebyll estate, it was leased by Herbert Lloyd, who remitted the rent as long as he lived. Memorial and foundation stones were laid by the Rt. Hon. Lord Glantawe (Sir John Jones Jenkins), Herbert Lloyd, Arthur Gilbertson, F.W. Gilbertson and Lewis Bowen, the last named being the oldest workman in the district. The Hall was used for local concerts and later as a cinema. The Institute (or 'Stute') consisted of a reading room, billiards hall, committee rooms and a house for the caretaker. It has recently been totally refurbished for use as an arts centre.

'Brynheulog', 1974. This was built in 1860 by Jacob Lewis (b. 1804) chemical manufacturer. He lived at Ynysygelynen House and it was his son, Lewis (1831-1920), who was recorded living at 'Brynheulog' in the 1861 census, along with Elizabeth his wife, son and two servants. It continued in the ownership of the Lewis family until the 1970s, the last resident member being Miss Elizabeth Lewis, daughter of Sidney (*c.* 1864-1958). The house was demolished 1978-79. Before 1860, the land had formed part of the Maes Iago estate of Philip Williams, master wool carder.

'Bryncelyn' in 1900. A pre-1877 establishment built on Tir y Bont land, this was initially the house of Griffith Griffiths, general medical practitioner and JP. In 1911, his son-in-law, Dr W.O. Evans, the son of the Revd John Evans of Gellionen Chapel, had a medical practice here, a tradition carried on by his son, Dr G.G.O. Evans ('Dr Geoff') until 1980.

GELLIONEN SPA-

SPA HOTEL.

THERE is now a commodious Hotel at Gellyonen Spa, at a short distance from the Pontardawe Station, on the Swansea Vale Railway, where every accommodation can be obtained.

Mr. WM. HUZZEY, Proprietor.—Conducted by Mr. and Mrs. MILLER.

ANALYSIS OF GELLIONEN WATER,

By Mr. Herapath, Bristol.

" In an Imperial Gallon there is contained in Grains and Decimal parts—

Organic Matters	.16
Chloride of Magnesium	.48
Chloride of Sodium	2.24
Sulphate of Magnesia	1.60
Carbonate of Lime..........	a trace
Bi-Carbonate of Iron	.80
Sulphate of Lime	.36
Total contents..	5.64

It will be seen that this is a very pure Spring, nearly free from Lime Sal·s; and that its principal medicinal quality is Chalybeate, as it possesses 8-tenths of a grain of Bicarbonate of Iron in a gallon. If the locality is salubrious and picturesque, it might be well to establish a Spa there."

The Trains leave Swansea three times a day for Pontardawe, and from the Ist of AUGUST a Train will leave Swansea on SUNDAYS at 2.15 p.m., returning from Pontardawe at 7.40, thus giving an opportunity to spend four hours at the Spa.

'The Spa' was the meeting place for those wishing to partake of the spa waters near Gellionen Chapel. It became popular after the opening of the Swansea Vale railway in 1860. Spa House was built around that time and was originally a hotel only later becoming a public house. It was uninhabited in 1861 but in the 1871 and 1881 censuses Rees Williams, a mason, was head. In 1891 it was headed by Thomas Gittens, farmer and licensed victualler. The hotel lost its licence in 1893 as the customers often picked rhododendrons from Arthur Gilbertson's gardens at 'Glanrhyd'. He was the chief magistrate!
The property has been owned by the Thomas family since 1920. Underground workings of the Daren Colliery had caused the spa waters to disappear completely by 1939.

Travellers Well, *c.* 1890. The publican at that time whose name is above the door was a 61-year-old land agent, David Lewis, who lived there with his wife, Ann, and four sons. He may be in the centre flanked by some of his sons and grandchildren. Pre-1838, in origin, the building is strategically placed at the junction of several highways.

Cross Hands public house, *c.* 1974, shortly before its demolition to make way for the new road pattern. It was of pre-1871 origin, being recorded for the first time in the census of that year with John Morgan, his wife Phoebe, eight children and son-in-law resident there. In 1881 and 1891, the publican was David Bowen.

Victoria Inn, *c.* 1890. The 'Vic' (renamed Kitty O'Shea's in 1995) is of pre-1871 origin and was built upon the site of Tyr Bont House which was owned in 1838 by Philip Williams of Maes Iago. It was one of the last public houses to be built in Pontardawe. In 1881, Hannah John was recorded as a beer-house keeper here and, in 1891, her husband Henry was named as publican. He was the son of Hopkin John of Ynysmeudwy Isaf and grandson of the 'ingenious and versatile' Shôn Ynysderw alias John Jones (1775-1851) of Ynysderw Farm.

Ynysmeudwy Arms public house, *c.* 1920. The landlord at that time was Evan John, related to Henry John of the Victoria Inn and to Hopkin John of Ynysmeudwy Isaf Farm. He was succeeded by his son, also Hopkin John, in the 1930s. The Ynysmeudwy Arms was originally Ynysmeudwy Uchaf farmhouse (constructed 1757) and was greatly enlarged sometime before 1875. The oldest part of the buildings is the portion nearest to the canal (to the left). The photograph also shows a group of tinplate workers from the Bryn tinplate works which was located close to the pub.

Trebanos post office, *c.* 1920. As can be seen, this grocery shop and post office was owned by Mr E. Thomas. In 1891 the proprietor had been Daniel Davies from Cilybebyll who lived here with his wife, son and daughter together with his mother-in-law and one servant. Note the boxes of oranges outside the shop which would eventually be utilised for sheds, fences and even furniture.

Alltwen Hill butcher's shop, *c.* 1900. This adjoined the Cross Hands Hotel and fronted what became the Alltwen Primary School lane. In 1891 David Jones was a butcher and dealer here and he is possibly pictured above with his wife, Ruth, son, John, and two other children. The other children named in 1891 were Hannah, Ivor, David, Phoebe, Claudia, Elias, Arthur and Mary. The property was demolished in the 1960s.

The Alltwen (top) and Pontardawe branches of the Alltwen and Pontardawe Co-operative Society Ltd. The Pontardawe branch was established in 1890 while the Alltwen one was opened in 1875 (in Gwyn Street, later moving to the sites at the Triangle and Alltwen Hill) and was the district's headquarters. The drapery, outfitting, bootwear, hardware and foodstore departments of the Pontardawe branch closed in the early 1980s. A decentralised housing office of the newly formed Neath Port Talbot County Borough Council has recently taken occupation of the Pontardawe site.

Cash & Co., *c.* 1950. This well-remembered shoe shop in Herbert Street closed in the mid-1950s. The assistant in the photograph is Enid James-Davies of James Street. The shop remained as a shoe shop until about 1977 by which time it was known as Turner's. It is now J. & S. Battenbough's paints and gifts shop.

Griffiths the tailor. William Griffiths was a tailor who lived and worked in Holly Street. He is seen here with his family *c.* 1880. In the 1881 census his son, John (back row, second from the right), is named as a tailor living in Orchard Street with his wife and two small children. He was aged 35 and had a nephew living with him as a journeyman tailor. Philip (with the long beard) was also a tailor in Banwen Cottages, Alltwen. Descendants of theirs still live in James Street.

The Cross, Pontardawe at the turn of the century with Davies the ironmonger's, centre. For sale, outside the building, are upturned copper wash-boilers which were often used as seats by the villagers of Pontardawe. The white building, to the left of the ironmonger's, is the Victoria Inn where David Gape was landlord in 1871. The old stone wall in front of the Victoria Inn is probably the boundary wall of the ancient house 'Tyr Bont' which was demolished to construct the inn. Far left is the Dynevor Arms public house erected about 1830. Note the absence of buildings along High Street.

Swansea Road, Pontardawe, 1908. The cottages centre right are Wesley Terrace where the poet, Gwenallt, was born in 1899. Beyond the cottages is No. 7 Swansea Road. The buildings were occupied by Jordan and Son, chemists, established in 1857, the London and Provincial Bank and the third of Pontardawe's post offices.

C. Williams 'Corn Stores' c. 1955. Ceinwen Williams (left) is in the doorway of her animal-feed shop at the bottom of James Street. She later moved across the road. This shop was until recently well known as the electricity showroom.

D J. Harries. This shop, a high grade grocery, was in High Street. It was one of many owned by the Harries family. It is currently occupied by Bleddyn Howells the butcher.

Richard Morgan, ironmonger and grocer, 1890. Along with Richard and Sarah Morgan, are their daughters, Gwennie (left), Jane (centre) and Elizabeth (right) holding Netta. The premises was later Arthur Evans, ironmongers (115 Herbert Street). It was demolished in the mid-1970s. Like Davies & Co., The Cross and W.J. Davies, Herbert Street, ironmongers supplied the works and the wider community with a variety of goods. Everything one wanted was in Arthur Evans's... somewhere!

James the Baker's, 117 Herbert Street, *c*. 1940. D.E. James set up a bakery here in the early part of this century. He married Gwennie, the daughter of Richard Morgan the ironmonger (above). It later became a general stores and remained in the family until the 1970s when like Arthur Evans's it was demolished. Many will recall the kindness and quality of service, provided by Jane, Dick, Hannah and Heber (pictured here).

Nine

Churches and Chapels

The district has a rich religious heritage. It was originally served by two 'ancient' parish churches – St Ciwg's, Llangiwg and St John the Baptist's, Cilybebyll. These remained the principal Anglican agencies until the second half of the nineteenth century when the growth of population and urbanisation necessitated the establishment of new churches: St Peter's (1860) and All Saints (1886) in Pontardawe and St John's (1886) in Alltwen. The process continued in the twentieth century with the erection of St Michael's and All Angels, Trebanos (1912) (in the parish of Clydach St John's) and St Mary's, Ynysmeudwy (1913). The area however has a very old dissenting tradition. The Unitarian chapel of Gellionen (one of the oldest in Wales) was originally erected in 1692 while the Independent causes at Baran and Gwrhyd were established in 1805 and 1856, respectively. Before the chapels were established, farmsteads had acted as meeting houses. Among these were Alltyfanog, Llachard Fawr, Llwyn Evan, Nantymoel Uchaf and Fforch Egel. Within the urban community most of the major denominations were represented – Baptist, Independent, Congregationalist, Calvinistic Methodist, Welsh Wesleyan Methodist, English Wesleyan Methodist, Unitarian, Apostolic and New Church. In all some twenty non-conformist chapels existed at one time and most survive today.

Llangiwg church, c. 1905. Founded in the sixth century by Ciwg an early Christian hermit who is said to be descended from a noble Celtic family. It stands 688 feet above sea level in a hollow on Barley Hill which was a central location before industrialisation took root in the valley below. The present building dates mainly from 1812 but parts of the tower are of thirteenth century origin. The leper window in the east was constructed so that 'unclean lepers' could view the priest celebrating communion. The ruins of the Maendy Inn (formerly the Cilybebyll Arms) remain nearby.

Cilybebyll church, *c.* 1950. Of twelfth century origin, the present building was substantially restored in 1869 by John Griffiths, contractor of Twyn y Morgrug, Alltwen. Built in the Norman style, it has seating capacity for 130. There are memorials inside the church to the Herberts and Lloyds of the Plâs. The registers date from 1776 and there have been twenty-one rectors since 1755.

Cilybebyll Rectory, 1903. By 1563 the church was considered to have assumed parochial status, the incumbent being John Bennett who is known to have lived near the church, perhaps in what is now the rectory, part of which is considered to go back at least four hundred years. In 1851, it was described as the 'Personag', William Thomas the 48-year-old rector living there. The rector from 1870 to 1905 was David Walter Jones, presumably pictured here (centre, standing).

Gellionen Chapel, *c.* 1910. This was erected in 1692 on Alltyfanog Farm land under the patronage of Bussy Mansel of Briton Ferry and was rebuilt in 1801 under the direction of the Revd Josiah Rees in the 38th year of his ministry. The chapel was erected after the Toleration Act of 1688 and the location that now appears remote would then have been the focal point of considerable traffic as several roads converge near this point. There was a large stable at the chapel where Josiah Rees is reputed to have kept a school. There have been some twenty-two ministers since 1692. A 'more convenient' chapel was opened in November 1894 at Capel y Graig, Trebanos.

Baran Chapel, 1977. Formerly the Trinitarian branch of Gellionen Chapel, when Gellionen went Unitarian the Independents left and for a year worshipped at Llwyn Evan Farm and subsequently Nantymoel Uchaf. In 1805, land was leased for five shillings a year from the latter and Baran Chapel established. Roger Howell of Nantymoel Uchaf was minister for its first 38 years. Baran had 181 members in 1841. Many farming families of the locality are buried there although worshippers came from far afield. The chapel was served by eight ministers up to 1974.

Tabernacle, Trebanos *c.* 1965. A Calvinistic Methodist chapel, it was built in 1842 on Graig Trebanos land at a cost of over £1,000 with seating for around 250 persons. The prime mover behind its establishment was the Revd John Walters. William Ivander Griffiths, the musician and ardent temperance champion was later appointed choirmaster here. The chapel closed *c.* 1971 and was demolished *c.* 1973.

Saron Congregational Chapel, *c.* 1930. The first services here date from 10 January 1844 when the minister was the Revd Rhys Price of Cwmllynfell. He was followed by John Jones, D.D. Walters, J. Jeffrey Evans and J.R. Price, under whose ministry membership increased and the new Saron chapel was opened nearby in 1904 with William Williams of Maesygwernen Hall, tinplate manufacturer and former MP, giving the land. The new chapel was built for £2,700. Both chapels were seemingly erected on Rhyd-y-fro Mill land.

Horeb, c. 1890. This Welsh Wesleyan chapel was opened in 1845 alongside what is now Glanrhyd Road. It and the adjoining vestry were built on Glynmeirch Farm land and were the result of a 600-year lease between Isaac Jones of Glynmeirch and John Lloyd, superintendent of the Wesleyan Methodist circuit. It was demolished and superseded by the new Horeb, opened in 1905 in James Street.

Pontardawe Cross, looking towards Horeb Chapel, James Street, c. 1910. There was accommodation for 500 when the new Horeb opened in 1905. Described as idiosyncratic Arts and Crafts Gothic, the chapel has a spray of wild typography on the upper façade. Among the other fascinating detail in this photograph are the Dynevor Arms (pre-1838) and the Victoria Inn (pre-1871). Opposite the 'Vic' is the original Waterfall Stores. The large building on the left, beyond, was a butcher's shop. Behind the Dynevor Arms is presumably the skating rink, built by L.W. Francis in 1909, which later became the Pavilion cinema.

Gwrhyd Chapel (Independent) was built for £350 in 1856 high on an exposed and lonely site (Cefn Gwrhyd) which abutted Gwrhyd Uchaf farm. Like Gellionen and Baran chapels it was once central for inhabitants who came on horseback or were accustomed to walking long distances. The building was enlarged in 1905. Two of the original deacons came from nearby farms – Hezekiah Evans of Gwrhyd Isaf and Llewellyn Rees of Gwrhyd Uchaf. The former schoolhouse lies to the left.

Alltwen Independent Chapel, *c.* 1910. Built on land leased from William Jones of Cilhendre Fawr, it was incorporated in 1757. The present chapel, seen here, was erected close to the old building in 1801. It was extended in 1814 and rebuilt 1831. The chapel was further extended in 1861 and rebuilt in 1886. The first vestry was built in 1858 and the present one (to the left) in 1893, the ground floor being used as a reading room until 1911. Also in this photograph is the Gwyn Hall (to the right of the chapel), The Rock public house and the Triangle (both pre-1838), the site in past times of the Alltwen Fair.

Bethesda Independent Chapel, Ynysmeudwy. This was built 1861-62 on land rented from the Ynysmeudwy Arms (formerly Ynysmeudwy Uchaf). The land was given 'for the purpose of erecting a small house to be used by the Calvinistic Dissenters or Congregationalists as a meeting place for Divine purpose'. The first Minister was the Revd Phillip Davies of Alltwen Chapel with whom it was linked. The chapel became too small to cater for the growing population and a new one was built near Curtis Row and opened in 1893. The old chapel was demolished in 1955.

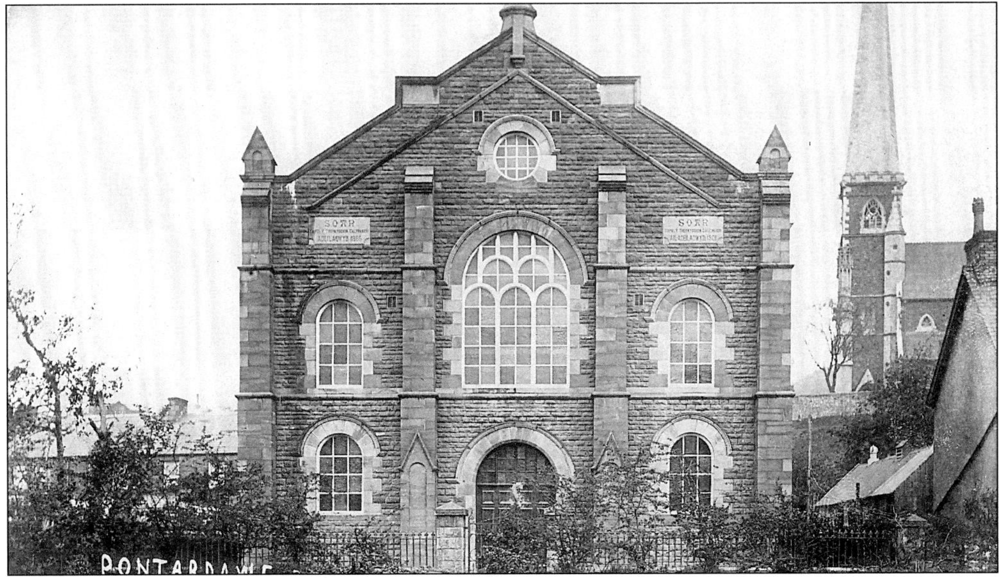

Soar Calvinistic Methodist, Holly Street *c.* 1913. It opened in 1866 on Cae Pandy, part of Ynysygelynen Farm land, with forty members. Rebuilt in 1901, it had upwards of 300 members by 1910. The first four ministers were John Edwards, William Morgan, Isaac Morgan and D.G. Jones, the latter serving for over forty years.

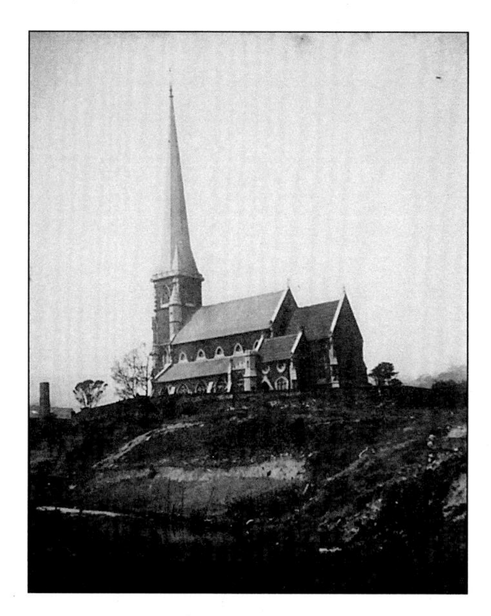

St Peter's church with its 197-foot spire. Built 1858-60 and consecrated in 1862, it was designed by J.H. Bayliss, built by J. Holtham, and erected on Tir y Bont land donated by Francis Edwardes Lloyd of Plâs Cilybebyll. William Parsons gave £5,557 towards the building cost. The Pontardawe Civic Society has installed permanent lighting to illuminate the church which is generously supported by voluntary donations. There have been twelve vicars since its foundation.

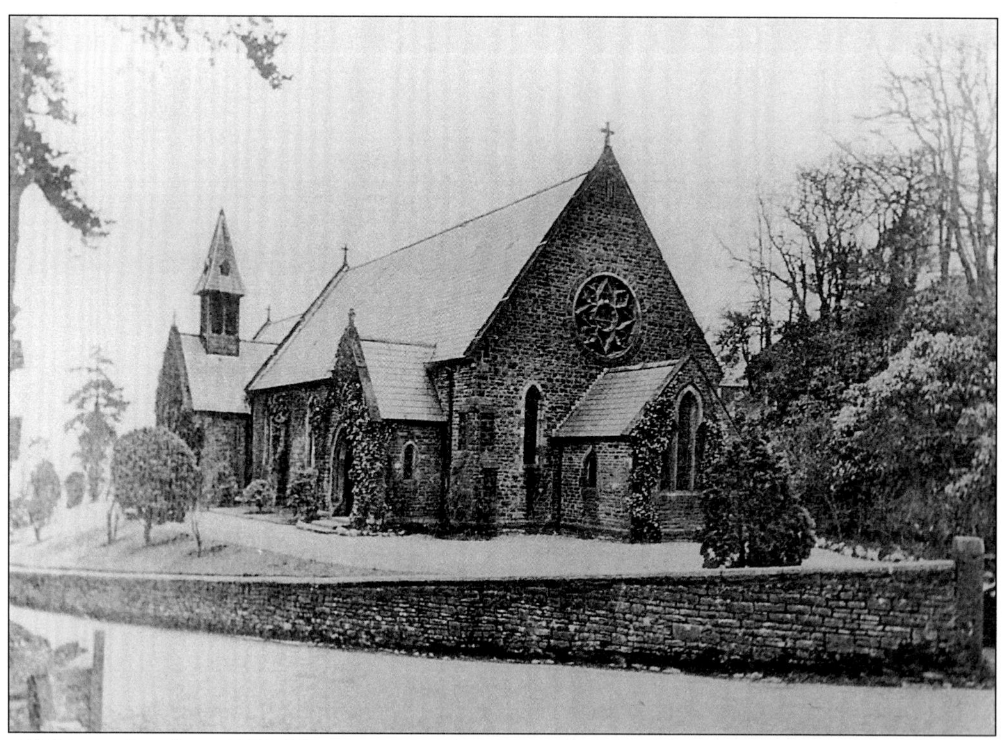

All Saints church, *c.* 1950. This was opened in September 1886 by Arthur Gilbertson who built it as a memorial to his father. It cost £2,440 with the land being donated by Herbert Lloyd, Plâs Cilybebyll (it lay on what had been Ynysderw Farm land). Owing to geological difficulties the church was constructed in a north-east direction by John Griffiths of Pontardawe. Originally in the parish of St John's, Clydach, it was transferred to the parish of Llangiwg in 1903.

St John the Baptist's, Alltwen, *c.* 1909. Built in 1886 overlooking Dyffryn Road on the Gwyn estate, it is the daughter church of St John's, Cilybebyll. It seats some 250 people and is built in the Victorian style. The first curate was the Revd D.J. Davies. A school house (the Gwyn Hall) was erected by Mrs Howel Gwyn in 1893 to hold Sunday school and social events (see p. 94).

Sunday school in the grounds of Whitland House in front of Bryn Seion *c.* 1905. The teacher is Rachel Lewis (*née* Davies), sister of the great-grandfather of Huw George (of Rhos), the donor of this photograph. Bryn Seion was built in 1896 as an offshoot of Alltwen Independent Chapel. Previously, services had been held in the nearby Gellinud Board School. The chapel is currently disused and for sale.

Tabernacle Sunday school in 1903 with (centre) teacher Morgan Morgan of George Street. Tabernacle Independent Chapel in Thomas Street was built by William George, Ystalyfera and John Griffiths, Pontardawe for £1,694. The foundation stone was laid by Sir John Jones Jenkins (later Lord Glantawe) on 18 August 1880 and officially opened on 21 August 1881. In 1890, a manse was built in Grove Road and a vestry in 1892. There were 360 members in 1911 and over 400 in 1963. Tabernacle has had a fine history as a cultural centre encouraging lectures, dramas and music.

Dosbarth Ysgol Sul Evan Williams, Saron, Rhyd-y-fro early 1930s. From left to right, standing: Anne Rees, Elizabeth Ann Jones, Ellen Davies, Mary Agnes Evans, Sarah Helen Jones, Mrs Ifan Thomas, Sarah Gwen Davies, Nellie Rees, Mrs John Haydn Davies; seated, middle: Annie Smith, Gemima Clement, Carrie Davies, Evan Davies (Penygoelan), Elizabeth Evans, 'Auntie Dianah', Miss Davies; front: Mary Ifor, Mrs Stephens.

Ten

Schools

The earliest school in the district was probably the one attached to Gellionen chapel (closed pre-1766). This preceded the circulating schools of Griffith Jones of Llanddowror which came to the parishes of Llangiwg in 1738 and Cilybebyll (Cwmnantllwyd) in 1746. There was a school at Baran chapel in 1805 and later at Nantymoel Uchaf in the 1820s but the first National (Anglican) school was at Cae'r Doc in 1830. This closed in 1847. Since then a number have been established to cater for the educational needs of the growing population. A church school was built in Brecon Road in 1856 which became a mixed National school in 1863. Other schools in Pontardawe and Ynysmeudwy included: the Rechabite Hall infants school 1866 (in 1873 the school moved to the 'Long Room' of the reading room, later the Lyric cinema); the Llangiwg mixed board school 1885 which became a girls' school in 1914 when the new boys' school was opened that year (the two amalgamated in 1964 to form the Llangiwg Primary School); Pontardawe Infants School (1899; Ysgol Gymraeg since 1969); the Zinc (Infants) School, Ynysmeudwy (1909); Ynysmeudwy Nursery School (1973-81); the higher elementary school (1913) which became a secondary grammar school in 1921; Pontardawe Technical College for Further Education (1934); the secondary modern school (1958) and Cwmtawe Comprehensive School (1969). In Cilybebyll parish, schools were opened at Plasywaun (1819), Penyralltwen (1839), Tanyrallt House (1870), Gellinudd (1874), 'The Ferns', Graig Road (c. 1880), Alltwen Infants (1883-4) and Junior (1903) and Rhos (1908). Rhyd-y-fro school was opened in 1876 (and one in Gwrhyd chapel in 1889). In Trebanos, Craig Trebanos school was opened in 1884 but replaced by new infants and junior schools in 1910 and 1915, respectively.

St Peter's school. Erected as a National school for boys and girls in 1857, the boys' schoolroom is to the right, the girls to the left, with a house attached for use of the head teacher. In 1859, there were 91 boys and 76 girls present. The buildings cost £1,276 18s 8d to construct, more than half the cost (£779) being met by public subscription and donations. In the external fabric of the building are a large amount of terracotta wares produced at Ynysmeudwy Pottery – the window surrounds, ridge crests, and roof wall cappings.

Pontardawe Collegiate School, Tanyrallt House. Established in 1870 on former Pontardawe (Flour) Mill lands, it provided private education for boys to sit external examinations for university and drew students from a wide area. The boys wore gowns and mortar boards, rode bicycles around Pontardawe and marched to St Peter's church for Sunday morning services. The principal was William Samuel, whose son Astley is recorded as living there in 1891 with his wife, four students, a French master and two servants. The college closed in 1896 and Astley Samuel became a Swansea auctioneer. Tanyrallt House is now a private nursing home having been a private residence for many years.

RHYBUDD.

I RIENI PLANT

YN

MHLWYF CILYBEBYLL.

Mae'r Bwrdd Ysgol yn dymuno arnoch yn ddifrifol i anfon eich Plant i'r Ysgol yn gyson. Achosir anghyfleusdra mawr mewn dysgu, a cholled i'r Plant eu hunain trwy ymbresenoliad afreolaidd.

Os na bydd i bob Plentyn fod yn bresenol 250 o weithiau, neu 125 o ddiwrnodau bob blwyddyn, bydd i'r Bwrdd golli Rhoddion y Llywodraeth. Rhaid i'r Bwrdd ragochelyd hyn er lles y Trethdalwyr.

Bydd yn rhaid i'r Bwrdd godi graddfa uwch o daliadau am y cyfryw nad ydynt yn *attendo* yn rheolaidd, ac os na bydd i hyn gynyrchu yr effaith dymunol, bydd y Bwrdd yn rhwym o ddodi yr Adran Orfodol mewn grym, pa un a'u galluoga hwynt i rwymo ymbresenoliad, trwy wysiad y Rhieni o flaen yr Ynadon.

Gobeithiwn na bydd yn rhaid i'r Bwrdd wneuthur hyn, ond bydd i chwi o'ch rhydd ewyllys eich hunain anfon eich Plant yn rheolaidd.

Arwyddwyd,

HERBERT LLOYD,
CADEIRYDD

HYDREF, 1874.

School attendance notice, 1874. Dated the same year the Gellinudd Board School was opened under the 1870 Education Act. The notice calls upon Cilybebyll parents to send their children to school regularly. It states that, unless a child attended school for over 250 half-days per year, the School Board would lose the government grant. The Board further state that a higher scale of fees would be charged for children who did not attend regularly. If that did not work the parents would be summoned before the magistrates to compel attendance.

Pontardawe Infants School, Thomas Street in 1913. This was built on Tir y Bont land owned by the Cilybebyll estate and was opened in 1899 by Principal Roberts of the University of Wales College of Aberystwyth. It had space for 250 children. In the first year, the average number of children who attended was 160 but by 1910 this had risen to 200. The first headmistress was Miss Hannah Jones MBE and she was followed by six others by the time the school became Ysgol Gymraeg in 1969.

Pontardawe Infants School interior, 1913.

Trebanos Infants School, 1929. The first school was erected in 1883 at Cae-is-Maen, Craig Trebanos and opened in 1884. It soon proved too small to accommodate the increasing number of children, however, and a new infants department was built in 1910 and in 1915 a junior department opened. The two amalgamated as Trebanos Primary School on 1 September 1964. The school has been closed since July 1993 because of subsidence fears. The original school continued for alternative uses until the 1980s but is severely dilapidated today.

Ynysmeudwy Infants School, 1910. The Zinc School built on Ynysmeudwy Ganol land, was opened in May 1909. It was constructed of zinc sheeting and internal wood panelling as a temporary structure but it was a tribute to the quality of material used that it was still structurally sound when demolished in 1969. A very popular and sentimental landmark, a nursery school was established on the site in 1973; this amalgamated with Llangiwg Primary School in 1981.

Rhyd-y-fro Infants School in 1931. Built in 1876, seemingly on Rhyd-y-fro Mill land, the first headmaster here was Mr A.W. Owen. The school closed in 1984, a new building having been constructed on Waun Penlan. A private nursing home (Cartref) incorporates the original building today.

Alltwen Junior School in 1910. Built in 1903, it superseded the previous school in Gellinudd (opened in 1874). The school accommodated 600 pupils, Mr George Jenkins being the first headmaster. It was built on Gwyn estate land. The infants school on Dyffryn Road was erected in 1883 on Tyn y Graig land with room for two hundred or more children. It closed in 1982 and is now a community centre.

Pontardawe Boys' School, 1920. Built on former Ynysmeudwy Isaf land, it was opened on 2 March 1914, 274 boys marching from the old school in Brecon Road to the new. The catchment area was from Pontardawe Cross to Cilmaengwyn and from Herbert Street to Gellygron. The first headmaster was J.J. Roberts, father of Percy Roberts, history master and later headmaster of Pontardawe Grammar School. It merged with the girls' school in 1964 to form Llangiwg Primary School.

Laboratory, Pontardawe Grammar School. Built on former Ynysmeudwy Isaf and Alltycham land, the Pontardawe Higher Elementary school opened on 6 September 1913 when 140 pupils enrolled. It became a secondary/grammar school in 1921, the first headmaster being John William Thomas. He was followed by four others up to 1969 when Cwmtawe Comprehensive School was formed. The latter, which also incorporated the Pontardawe Technical College and the secondary modern school, has recently moved (September 1996) to a new site on Parc Ynysderw.

Eleven

Personalities

The district has seen or given rise to a variety of personalities from all walks of life. Those included here represent an 'eclectic' choice as readers will soon appreciate.

William John Evans, 'Will Asbestos'. A great character from Fuller Street. He was foreman of the annealing furnace in the sheetworks where he was employed from at least 1936. He was, like many of his contemporaries, a very hard worker who would 'walk through fire'. He would pull sheets stuck in the furnace out with his hands. His clothes would be on fire and he would jump in the cooling trough and wouldn't have a mark. One of his sons was Dewi Evans who worked in the steelworks fitting shop, one of many father and son combinations who 'worked in the works'.

Rachel Thomas (1905-95). 'No Welsh actress past or present has been revered as much in her own country as Rachel Thomas' (David Berry). Born in Alltwen, she lived at 'Tyle Coch', a name she was to give to her residence at Rhiwbina so attached was she to her home and place of origin. A star of radio, film and television, her first film was *The Proud Valley* (1940). In the 1950s and 1960s, Rachel came into her own both on radio and as a screen actress, forging her familiar image of the firm but doting mother ('Mam') who often kept her family afloat. She played Mrs Lloyd in *The Valley of Song* (1953) and Beth Morgan in *How Green Was My Valley* (BBC, 1960), a far superior performance to that of Sara Allgood in the 1941 Hollywood version. Her last screen role was in *Whistling Boy* (BBC Wales, 1994), shown a few weeks before her death.

Harriet Lewis. A native of Trebanos she has spent all her working life in the teaching profession being a head teacher for 25 years. She started a Welsh junior school in Pontardawe in 1967 (Ysgol Gywradd Gymraeg) the lessons being held in the vestry of Tabernacle Chapel. A very popular lay preacher she has also worked successfully as a professional actress in radio and television rubbing shoulders with such legends as Ivor Novello, Gwen Ffrancon Davies, Sir Geraint Evans and Sir Anthony Hopkins. Although Harriet prefers 'straight' roles, it is in the field of comedy that she is best known, particularly in the medium of Welsh. Early radio series include *Siop y Gornel* and *Peidiwch a Sôn* but today she is best known as 'Maggie Post' in television's *Pobol y Cwm*, now in its twenty-seventh year. Harriet hopes to carry on acting until the end.

David James Jones ('Gwenallt'). Born in Wesley Terrace in 1899, this poet, critic, scholar and Christian pacifist was a conscientious objector during the First World War and sent to Wormwood Scrubs and Dartmoor for refusing to fight. He won the chair at the 1926 National Eisteddfod for his *awdl* 'Y Mynach'. He repeated the feat in 1931 for 'The Poet's Dream'. His childhood and adolescence in a Welsh-speaking, chapel-going, industrial community in the shadow of the steel and tinplate works were vividly evoked in his contribution to the volume of autobiographical essays, *Credaf* (ed. J.E. Meredith, 1943). His reputation however rests chiefly on a number of shorter poems contained in his five volumes of poetry *Ysgubau'r Awen* (1939), *Cnoi Cil* (1942), *Eples* (1951), *Gwreiddiau* (1959) and the posthumous *Coed* (1969). He died in 1968.

Dafydd Rowlands, poet, prose writer and current Archdruid of Wales. Born in 1931 in Pontardawe, he was educated at University College, Swansea and the Presbyterian College, Carmarthen. A minister at Brynamman and a school master before becoming a lecturer in Welsh at Trinity College, Carmarthen (1968). He won the Crown at the National Eisteddfod in 1969 and the Prose Medal in 1972. He has published a lecture on Gwenallt and edited a volume on that poet. His other works include *Meini* (1972), *Yr Wythfed Dydd* (1975), *Paragraffau o Serbia* (1980), *Licyris Olsorts* (1995) and *Sobers a fi* (1995). He now lives in Rhos.

Teddy Morgan (left), being offered good wishes before leaving for Spain to take up an appointment as pit foreman in a steelworks, *c.* 1954. Teddy had worked in the Pontardawe steelworks' casting pit. In the centre is Wynne Meredith (melting shop manager) and, right, Tom Canning, steelworks manager.

Many a head of hair was cut by John ('Jock') McDade seen here outside his shop at Pontardawe *c.* 1974 (part of Motor World Ltd today). He hailed from Montrose and married Winifred Ayres on 20 September 1944 at St Peter's church, the year he started his hairdressing business in Pontardawe. He retired in the mid-1970s and died in 1992 aged 81. His contemporary hairdressers in the 1950s and 1960s were Jack Hughes (Herbert Street), Gwilym Williams (Dynevor Terrace) and Richard John Jenkins (High Street).

George Holloway. Known to Pontardawe people as 'Georgie Canal', he was the lengthsman on the Pontardawe to Ynysmeudwy section of the Swansea Canal (1919-1950s). George was born at Ludlow and came to Pontardawe after being demobbed from the army in 1919. He started working on the canal in that year, his first job being the erection of fencing alongside the canal at Ynysmeudwy. George lived at Carpenters Row in Pontardawe and is seen here in a canal maintenance boat at Ynysmeudwy Ganol bridge in 1929. The boat contains tree branches that the maintenance men have removed which were overhanging the canal. In the background under the bridge arch is one of the Waun Coed cottages.

Dan Morgan, outside Gellygron Mill, *c.* 1926. Known locally as 'Dan y Felin', he lived at Mill Farm, formerly Tir Shet. The Morgan family had been in possession of the mill for many years. Dan had three brothers who were millers: David Morgan of Neuadd Mill, Garnant; Thomas Morgan, Whitland and Abraham Morgan, Ystalyfera.

Tom Howell, born in The Ropewalk, Neath in 1890 (d. 1970). In the words of J.R. Jones he was 'one of the great stalwarts of Pontardawe Rugby, who gave the club over 50 years of service, first as a player and then as a coach, committeeman and groundsman and marvellously still found time to become one of Wales's leading Rugby referees'. His son, Trevor (b. 1918), has followed in his father's footsteps and given selflessly to the local rugby and cricket clubs over many years.

Will Hopkin, *c.* 1910. Born at Rhydygwin, Craig Cefn Parc in 1882, he was educated at Clydach and Ynystawe elementary schools and later at Pontardawe Collegiate School, Alltwen under Astley Samuel. In 1900, he joined the *Cambrian Daily Leader* but left for the USA in 1908, returning in 1910. He started-up the *West Wales Observer* in 1919 and was also one of the founders of the South Wales and Monmouthshire Association of Newspaper Proprietors and President of the region's Guild of Editors and Branch Institute of Journalists. He died in 1968.

J.E. Morgan was born in Rhos but later lived in Edward Street, Alltwen. His bardic name was 'Hirfryn'. He wrote the first official history of Pontardawe – *Hanes Pontardawe* – which began as an essay for an eisteddfod in the Public Hall and was published in 1911. Previously, in 1908, he had published *Hen Gymeriadau Gellinudd* ('Old Characters of Gellinudd'), also after winning an eisteddfod, this time at Bryn Seion. The latter contains wonderful descriptions and stories of the people who had lived in the village. Excellent translations of both books have been provided by Ivor Griffiths.

Griffith Griffiths of 'Bryncelyn', a general medical practitioner. Born in 1840, he was the son of the Revd Phillip Griffiths of Tyn y Cae Farm, Alltwen, who gave 60 years service to Alltwen chapel. Educated at University College, Swansea and University College Hospital, London, he was a member of the BMA and JP for Glamorgan. He married Elizabeth Whittington in 1865. His one daughter, Gwladys, married Dr W.O. Evans and they were the parents of Dr G.G.O. Evans (d. 1985).

Josiah Rees. He was born in Llandovery in 1744, the son of the Revd Owen Rees of Aberdare. During Josiah's long ministry at Gellionen chapel (1764-1804), the congregation became Arminian, Arian and semi-Unitarian. Josiah was a founder member of the Welsh Unitarian Society whose first official meeting was held at Gellionen in 1802. He lived at Gellygron House, where he had a famous library, and died in 1804. His son, Dr Thomas Rees succeeded him at Gellionen. Another son, Owen, became a founder member of Longman's (publishers) while Josiah the younger was the owner of Gellygron and adjoining farms in 1838.

Howel Gwyn (1806-88). He owned much of Alltwen which his father, William (1766-1830), had purchased from the Briton Ferry estate in 1821. Among the acquisitions were Cilhendre Fawr and Fach, Alltwen Isaf, Ganol and Uchaf and Tyn y Cae. Gwyn Street, the Gwyn Arms and Gwyn Hall reflect this link today as does Dyffryn Road which was presumably named after the mansion Gwyn bought at Bryncoch in 1853. As well as being MP and High Sheriff, he held many high offices in local government and on behalf of statutory undertakings. He also founded many churches and schools. He married Ellen Elizabeth Moore in 1851 and when she died in 1900 the estate devolved to her nephew, Joseph Moore-Gwyn (1850-1922), four of whose children married Gilbertsons.

Twelve

Leisure

Our part of the Swansea Valley has always scored highly in terms of cultural endeavour, notably in the fields of poetry, prose and music. As well as Gwenallt and Dafydd Rowlands, both of whom are covered elsewhere, among the district's most famous sons is Ben Davies, the world renowned international tenor of the late nineteenth and early twentieth centuries. The district also has a fine choral and instrumental heritage perhaps the most famous choir of yesteryear being that established by William Ivander Griffiths between 1860 and 1870. There has also been a vibrant local Welsh folk scene over many years represented in more recent times by the Valley Folk Club (founded 1966) and the Pontardawe International Music Festival.

In addition, the district has a rich if underrated sporting and recreational tradition. All manner of sports have been followed and not only well-known ones like rugby, association football, cricket and golf. Boxing too has been significant – the names of Ronnie James and Bryn 'Ginger' Jones spring readily to mind – while other activities such as tennis, athletics, bowls, cycling, hockey, billiards, snooker, table tennis, angling and archery have been enthusiastically pursued. The Gilbertsons, in particular, were energetic promoters of sport as well as active participants. The Scout and Girl Guide movements have also been important while a variety of clubs and societies have flourished over the years. Facilities for reading, adult and community education, roller skating, concerts, theatre and cinema going have also been available.

Benjamin Grey Davies, one of the most famous of Welsh singers, was born in Herbert Street on 6 January 1858. His father died seven years later and his mother, penniless with four children, moved to Cwmbwrla. He won an eisteddfod at Swansea and shortly afterwards was heard by Brinley Richards, the composer, who advised him to study at the Royal Academy where he won the gold medal and became an associate. He joined the Carl Rosa Company and made his debut in *The Bohemian Girl* at Bristol in 1881. He created the title role in Sullivan's *Ivanhoe* in 1891 for which he was said to have been paid the highest amount ever for a British tenor on the stage. He toured the USA thirteen times as well as Germany, Australia and Africa. He made well over a hundred records and sang extensively at concerts and festivals. His last recordings were made in 1933 and he died on 28 March 1943 in Bristol.

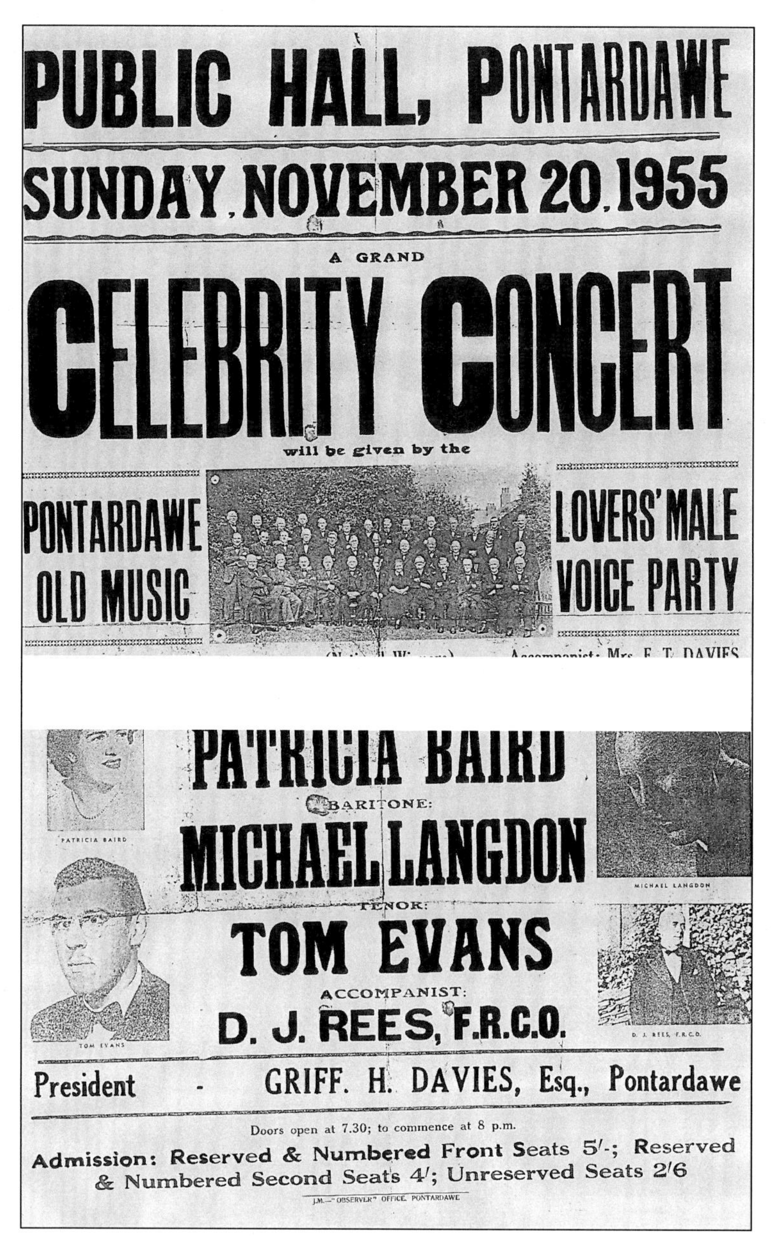

Two famous products of Pontardawe are featured on this poster for a concert in the Public Hall in 1955. The first is the Pontardawe Old Music Lovers' Male Voice Party. This was a choir for 'old age pensioners' and had an average age of 75. It was formed in 1945 and survived until at least 1959. They won the National Eisteddfod when it was held in Ystradgynlais in 1954. Their conductor was Evan T. Davies. They rehearsed twice a week in the steelworks canteen and their annual celebrity concerts at the Public Hall aided the Swansea Blind Institution. The second is Tom Evans the well known tenor, bottom left. He started singing after being known as 'The Singing Bus Conductor'. Locally he was in great demand and sang for many opera groups. He was offered a chance at Covent Garden but, for personal reasons, had to turn it down.

Wilfred Pickles' *Have a Go* show in the Public Hall, 11 May 1951. Among those in the audience are Iris Evans Davies, Lou Annie Thomas, Gwen Tweedy, Mrs Tawe Thomas, Catherine Carney, Mrs Albert Evans, Gertie Francis, Joan Jenkins Jones, Gwyneth Davies, Mrs Teddy James, Enid James, Margaret Rees-Sutton, Betty Thomas, Mary Thomas, Noah Davies, Mrs John and Mrs Griffiths (sisters of Quarr Road) and Mrs Jones (Orchard Street). Were you there?

PAVILION CINEMA
PONTARDAWE
A. J. LEWIS—Manager. Phone: Pontardawe 3104
MONDAY, OCTOBER 11
GREER GARSON - WALTER PIDGEON
in
Mrs. MINIVER
The Film supreme of Britain's Darkest, but Finest Hour
In Technicolor — Also —
Bonita Granville in THE LIE DETECTOR
THURSDAY, OCTOBER 14
LESLIE HOWARD - WENDY HILLER
in
PYGMALION
Bernard Shaw's Masterpiece
— Also —
THE CAT CREEPS
Admission: 1/-, 1/9 & 2/3 (including Tax)
Daily 4-30 to 10 p.m. Saturdays from 4 p.m.
Free Car Park for Patrons

Each Evening from 5 p.m. till 10
PHONE: 2256
THE LYRIC
Saturdays from 4 o'clock
Monday, October 11.
Betty Grable, Carmen Miranda
John Payne, E. Horton in
SPRINGTIME IN THE ROCKIES
Technicolor — Also —
Jack Train as Col. Chinstrap in
WHAT'S YOURS
PICTORIAL LATEST NEWS
Thursday, October 14.
Jean Pierre Aumont, Jean Hopkins
Cecil Parker, Margaretta Scott in
THE FIRST GENTLEMAN
— Also —
WEDDING BELLS
TALE IN A TEA CUP
LATEST NEWS

Each Evening from 5 p.m. till 10
PUBLIC HALL
Saturdays from 4 o'clock
Monday, October 11.
Jane Russell, Louis Hayward
Faith Domergue, Kent Taylor in
YOUNG WIDOW
— Also —
William Boyd, Andy Clyde in
DANGEROUS VENTURE
PICTORIAL LATEST NEWS
Thursday, October 14.
Cornel Wilde, Anita Louise
Henry Daniell, Russell Hicks in
The Bandit of Sherwood Forest
— Also —
Richard Dix, Barton McLane in
Mysterious Intruder
LATEST NEWS

Pontardawe cinemas, October 1948. In its heyday, Pontardawe had three cinemas – The Pavilion in Church Street, the Public Hall and The Lyric in Herbert Street. The Pavilion (originally a skating rink) closed in 1957 and was demolished in 1963 and the Berlei factory erected on the site 1964. The Public Hall closed in 1962 and became a bingo hall. The Lyric (formerly The Palace) was originally a reading room (opened in 1869), later becoming a Rechabite hall and concert hall. It closed as a cinema in 1970 with the premises later being occupied by Swansea Valley Carpets. In 1995, this premises was converted into flats on the upper floor with a chemist shop on the ground floor.

Mary Hopkin. She was born in 1950, the daughter of Betty and the late David Howel Hopkin, Chief Housing Officer with the Pontardawe Rural District Council. Educated at Pontardawe Grammar School, her first television appearance was on *Heddiw* (1966). She also appeared in *Hob y Deri Dando* in February 1968 before achieving international fame later that year with the release of *Those Were The Days*. She made several recordings for Cambrian Records, Pontardawe and was elected to the bardic circle in 1970 for her contribution to folk music. Mary now lives near Henley-on-Thames and has two grown-up children, Delaney and Jessica. Her main musical interest today is composing. Her sister Carole is also widely respected in the locality as a writer, artist and actress.

Dance display by Dawnswyr Treforus, a traditional Welsh dance team formed in 1977, seen here encouraging spectator involvement on the dance floor at Pontardawe Folk Festival in 1979. Sharon Blakesley of Brecon Road is the dancer, centre right. Dawnswyr Treforus were National Eisteddfod and Llangollen dance-team winners during the late 1970s and early 1980s. Beginning in 1977, the first festivals were held very close to the village at the top of Francis Street where Somerfield's car park is at present. The event became an international music festival in 1984 and introduced Pontardawe to music from all over the world.

Pontardawe Festival, early 1980s. Max Boyce (centre), seen here on the festival field, used to sing at the Valley Folk Club at the Ivy Bush, Pontardawe, during his early days as a folk singer. Alongside Max (right) is Ieuan Lewis the former Chief Public Health and Shops Inspector of Pontardawe RDC. He was a great supporter of the Festival and all things that brought Pontardawe to life.

'Yr Hwntws', one of the leading Welsh folk groups of the 1970s and 1980s at the Pontardawe Folk Festival in 1983. They were a five-piece band that sang traditional and contemporary songs in Welsh and English. The line-up in 1983 was, from left to right: Danny Kilbride, bass guitar; Jethro Newton, bodhran and vocals; Greg Lynn, twelve-string guitar. Not shown were Paul Hopkins, bouzouki, fiddle and mandolin and Brian Stafford, uillean pipes.

Golf Club ball at the Rink in 1948. Among those present are, back row: Ivor Harris, Haydn Davies, Ronnie Williams, John and Eleanor Gibbs, Phyllis Davies, Dilys Davies, T J. Thomas. Middle row: Mr and Mrs Conway Jenkins, Stanley Griffiths, Mr and Mrs Len Hodgkish, Coleen Davies, Bryn Davies, T.J. Morgan, John Davies, Lorna Griffiths, Mary Jones and Florrie Webb. Front row: Gwyneth Williams, Tony Hudson, Ceinwen Williams, Phil Michael, Cissie Williams, Mrs Dr Trevor Jenkins, Gladys Morgan, Doris Morgan. Dr Trevor Jenkins is seated on the floor.

Scouts of the 3rd Swansea Valley Troop, Pontardawe pulling their cart c. 1920. The lad on the extreme right is Morgan Evan Jones who lived at Tabernacle House, Trebanos. He went to London for the Jamboree in 1920 and later became a scout master.

Swimming in Cwmdu. Pontardawe's unemployed men constructed this swimming pool in Cwmdu in 1935. This photograph shows the Gala Day that year. Other pools were built for women and children. The pool was dammed using railway lines and large stones and was up to 12-feet deep. The pools became the village social centre during many subsequent summers. In the photograph can be seen Howard Lewis on the diving board, Ellis Jeremiah preparing to dive from the tree stump, Tommy Lewis standing top left with hands in pockets and Mr J.R. Williams seated in front on the extreme right.

Fishing in Cwmdu, c. 1903. The beautiful waterfall in Cwmdu is the backdrop for this lone fisherman and his audience. Large trout have been commonly taken from the Glen now that it is unpolluted by the coal washeries of Abernant. Charles Gilbertson presented the Glen to the community in the mid-1950s and a great deal of conservation has been undertaken in recent years.

Pontardawe and District Angling Society, 1950s. Bryn 'Ginger' Jones (centre) tries to convince Charles and Ellen Gilbertson that it really was a big one! To the right of 'Ginger' is Gerwyn Griffiths (chemist). Others included are Dr Richards, Len Edwards, Howard Hopkins, Geoff Stock and Dr Stan Hill (back, right). Gilbertson was Life President of the society, founded in 1947.

Pontardawe Archery Club at the Recreation Ground, mid-1950s. Among those shown are Jack Thomas (back, left), Wynne Meredith (centre of photograph) and Tom Howell (second from the right). A key member of this group, though not shown, was George Exell.

Bryn 'Ginger' Jones. Born at Ammanford in 1905, he was undefeated Welsh featherweight boxing champion between 1929 and 1934. He also fought and lost to Al 'Panama' Brown, world bantamweight champion (1929-1935) though Brown was no longer world champion at the time. 'Ginger' subsequently became an insurance agent and was a member of the Pontardawe Branch Lodge of the Loyal Order of the Moose. He was a likeable and very well-known personality. He died in 1986.

Ronnie James. Born at Bonymaen in 1917, he came to live at Cilhendre Fawr Farm in 1940. He was undefeated British lightweight champion (1944-47), having beaten Eric Boon for the title in August 1944 at Cardiff Arms Park in front of 35,000 fans. He was defeated by Ike Williams for the world lightweight title in September 1946 at Ninian Park when the black American tore him apart with tremendous bolo punches to the body. His last fight was against Cliff Curvis in June 1947, Curvis stopping him in seven rounds. All told, Ronnie took part in 116 contests, winning 95 (he drew 5 and lost 16). He always insisted on wearing the same pair of boxing shorts seen here. He wore these for all 116 contests he fought. Ronnie subsequently became a boxing promoter before emigrating to Australia where he died in 1977.

Ron Harries from Trebanos, *c.* 1932. An all-round athlete, Ron was Welsh champion in the 100 and 200 yards, hurdles, high jump and pole vault between 1931 and 1940. He played first-class rugby for Neath and Llanelli, as well as for Pontardawe and Trebanos, and was also a versatile performer in other spheres, being an accomplished artist, cartoonist, step dancer, stage and film star. A very generous character always keen to help aspiring athletes and sportsmen, he died in 1995, aged 83.

Judith Foston (*née* Evans), left, won over 100 full caps for Wales in hockey and was an accomplished performer. Born in 1954, she was educated at Pontardawe Grammar and Cwmtawe Comprehensive schools and Caerleon Training College. She gained her first cap in March 1974, took part in the world championships of 1975 and represented Great Britain at the 1984 Olympics. To her left is Marilyn Pugh (*née* Morgan) and Margaret Rainbow. Her brother, Baden, was also an all-round sportsman excelling at rugby.

Jessie Leyshon, Welsh ladies bowls international. She began as a member of the Victoria Park Club, Swansea 1964 later representing Glamorgan and Wales. Jessie lives at Riverside Court, Pontardawe and still plays indoors at the Pontardawe Leisure Centre.

The Glanrhyd Tennis Club, *c.* 1905. Seated centre, is Charles Gilbertson who was a great supporter of the game. There were courts at both Glanrhyd and Gellygron. Bottom right is Phil Hopkin, a supreme athlete, being a full rugby union international as well as a skilful soccer and hockey player, an accomplished runner and golfer. He was also a brilliant tennis player being Gilbertson's doubles partner. Also included are from left to right, back row: -?-, S. Edmunds, A. Davies (ironmonger's on The Cross), C. Giddings and W. Llewelyn.

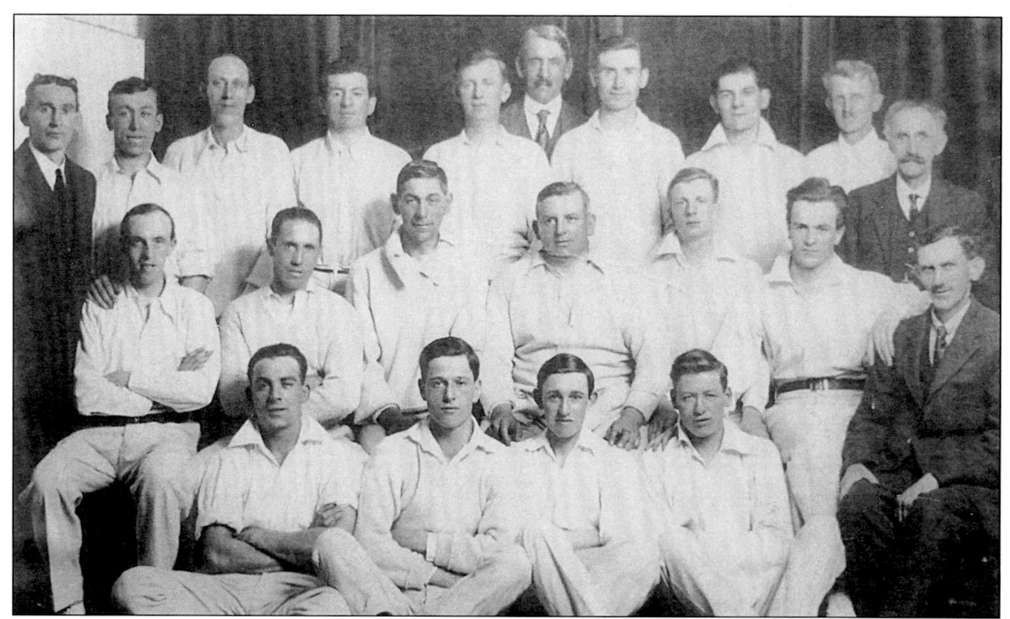

Pontardawe Cricket Club on their tour of Somerset and North Devon in August 1924. From left to right, standing: H. Williams, W. Budd, A.B. Suff, W.J. Bevan, B. Thomas, D. Bowen, S.V. Thomas, R.H. Lewis, W. Palmer, J.C. Jones. Middle: D.W. Suff (hon. secretary), E. Suckling, R.M. Lewis, E. Bevan (captain), C. Bubb, R. Thomas, W.D. Evans (umpire). Bottom: E. Davies, E. Thomas, A.G. Suff (scorer), J. Lewis. The club was formed in 1866, the same year as Ystalyfera.

Pontardawe Cricket Club in 1934 when they were champions of the South Wales and Monmouthshire Cricket Association Division 1 and winners of the Dan Radcliffe Challenge Cup. From left to right, standing: D.W. Suff (hon. secretary), L. Evans, R. Williams, C. Powell, R. Morris, W. Jones, T.A. Vaughan, W.T. Jones, O.S. Thomas (scorer). Seated B. Thomas (vice- chairman), C. Bubb, F. Roberts, W.F. Gilbertson (captain), A.G. Suff, W.M. Jones, W.T. Thomas (hon. treasurer). Insets: C. Pittman, G. Hopkins.

Pontardawe Association Football team in 1895, captained by Cecil F. Gilbertson, third from the right in the front row. This was the works eleven which later became the Gilbertsons Welfare team. It survived up to the Second World War fielding sides in the Swansea and District and Neath and District leagues. Pontardawe Athletic was formed in 1946 and initially played in the Neath and District League. In 1948/9 they joined the Second Division (West) of the Welsh League. Their survival owed much to the secretary, J.R. (Jackie) Williams, who organised the games, held the flag and acted as trainer. They were promoted to the first division for the first time in 1961. Currently, they are in the second division of the Welsh League.

Alltwen RFC, *c.* 1919, the year it is said to have been founded. Known initially as 'The Canaries' the club subsequently became the 'All Blacks'. For many years it played in the Swansea and District League but became a member of the West Wales Rugby Union and now plays in the Welsh National League. Its headquarters is the former Rock public house. Matches were once played on a field leased from Cilhendre Fach but in recent years the club has moved to a new pitch on what was Tyn y Cae land.

Pontardawe RFC, 1903-04 season. The club was formed in 1881 and in its early years was a match for Swansea, Neath and Llanelli. Matches were played at the old recreation ground that lay between the canal and Francis Street. From left to right, back row: L. Thomas, S. Daniel, S. Mathias, D.J. Thomas, L.W. Francis, J. Carney; second row: D. Watkins, J. Seddon, W. Smith, M. Thomas, A. Williams, W. Lewis, G. Smith, E. Morgan, J.D. Thomas, F. Scale; third row: T. Rees, J. Watkins, D. Daniel, W. Rees, F. Davies, D. Morgan; front: T. Lewis, F. Vaughan, B. Duncan.

Pontardawe RFC, 1909-10 season. From left to right, back row: B.I. Phillips, W. Dodd, R. Hendy, W. Evans, J. Wilcox, J.T. Davies; second row: J.D. Thomas, D. Jones, D. Davies, H. Rees, S. Morgan, T.J. Williams, W. Morgan, D. Thomas, W. Webb, S. Daniels; third row: J. Thomas, A. Williams, F. Vaughan, J. Davies, T. Lewis, W. Kift, G. Williams, G. Smith; front: T. Rees, D. Thomas, J. Rapsey, W. Symonds. The 'Cherry and Whites' have produced four full Welsh caps: Phil Hopkin, Edgar Morgan, Bryn Lewis and Gwilym Michael.

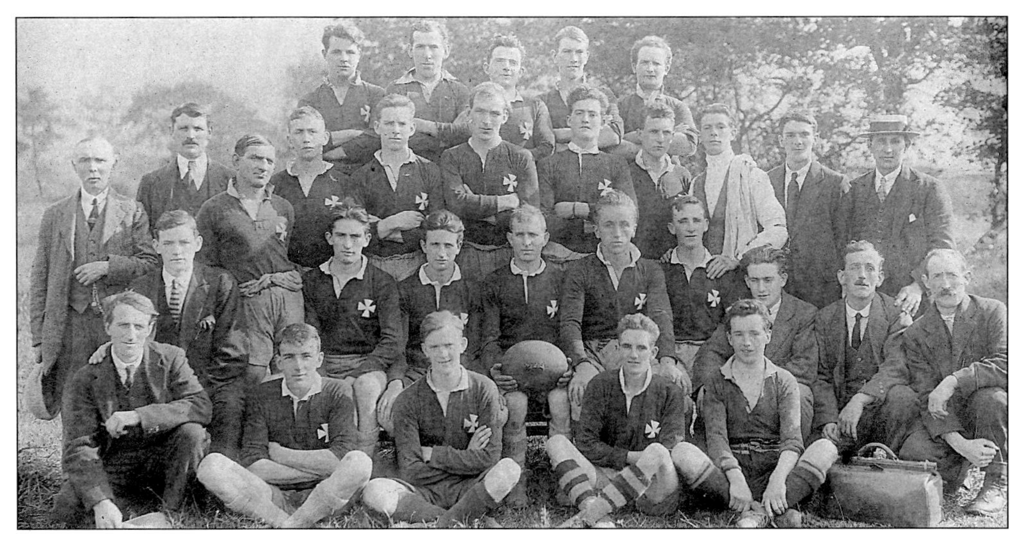

Trebanos RFC, 1922-23. From left to right, top row: T.J. Chudleigh, A. Davies, J. Bowen, T.J. Walters, J.L. Rees; third row: L. Ford, T.H. Jones, L.D. Davies, J.E. Lewis, D. Davies, W. Davies, W. Bale, L. Williams, W.E. Lloyd, D.E. Lloyd, E. Thomas; second row: D.G. Thomas, S. Evans, D.J. Lloyd, J. Davies, D.R. Lloyd, W.J. Bowen, T.J. Bale, E. Lloyd, D. Jones; bottom row: W.D. Bowen, J.H. Hopkins, W.R. Williams, T.J. Lewis, J.O. Morgan. Formed in 1897, the club flourished for the next 52 years in the Swansea and District League before being awarded full WRU status in 1949. In recent years the club has produced full internationals in the persons of Bleddyn Bowen, Robert Jones and Arwel Thomas.

RTB's (Richard Thomas and Baldwin's) fifth and last children's party, Christmas 1961. Among the happy children are David and Pat Jeremiah, Avril Jones, Jeff Childs, Eleanor, Alice and Gwendoline Howell. Monitoring the situation is Gwen Pugh (top left). Are you there?

Acknowledgements

Special acknowledgements to:

Mary Hopkin for kindly agreeing to write the foreword; Nannette Pearce (née Gilbertson) for supplying so much material on the Gilbertson family; Matthew Kidwell for also furnishing Gilbertson material and for his comments on the Gilbertson text; Joan and the late R.J.H. Lloyd for providing the Lloyd, Leach and Herbert of Plâs Cilybebyll images; Susan Beckley, County Archivist, West Glamorgan Archive Service, for allowing the reproduction of the images on pages 11, 57(a) and 100(b); The Ordnance Survey for giving permission for the reproduction of the maps on pages 12, 13 & 14; Simon Eckley, of Chalford Publishing, for his encouragement and support.

We also wish to thank everyone who kindly loaned photographs or provided help in other ways. We were overwhelmed by the enthusiastic support given to us.

Photographs provided by:

Dai Burgin; Cliff Curvis; D.W. Davies; Ben Davies; David T. Davies; Delyth Davies; Howel Davies; Huw Ebenezer; Irene Evans; John Evans; Tom Evans; Nancy Exell; Ruth Exell-Stevenson; Noire Frame; Huw George; Doreen Griffiths; Lee Hanford; Derek Harper; John Hills; Betty Hopkin; Aldwyn James; Gwen James; Mrs Ronnie James; William J. James; Elwyn & Helen Jenkins; Paul Jenkins; Eira Jones; Frank Jones Collection; Hannah Jones; Jane Jones; Mike Jones; Philip Jones; Bryn Lewis; Carol and Keith Lewis; Harriet Lewis; the daughters of Thomas Aldwyn Lewis; Len Ley; Jessie Leyshon; Thomas Lloyd; Rob Merril; Ian Milne; Diana Parker; Pontardawe International Music Festival; Pontardawe RFC; Edwina Ranft; Teifion Rees; Ann Roderick; Swansea Canal Society; Swansea Valley Historical Society; Steve Thomas; Maureen Todd; Trebanos RFC; Graham Williams; Tal Williams; Mr and Mrs Williams, Brecon Road; Ian Wright.

Information and assistance from:

Peggy Allan; Mrs J. Allen-Mirehouse; Mair Bale; Ann Barnard; Eirwen Bowen; Graham Cadwalladr; Howel Childs; Joan Childs; Cilybebyll Community Council; Gwyn Davies; Michael Duggan; Beth Edwards; Ailsa Evans, Mrs G.G.O. Evans, Phyllis Evans; Ron Firth; Diana Gilbertson; Elizabeth Gilbertson; Mark Gilbertson; Col. R.H. Gilbertson, W.F. Gilbertson; David Griffiths; Hilda Griffiths; Ivor Griffiths; John Griffiths; Wynne Griffiths; Barbara Grove; Mrs Ray Howell; Beryl Jenkins; William Jenkins; Alec John; Betty Jones; Eunice Jones; J.R. Jones; Myra Jones; Nora Jones; Tom Jones; John Lewis; Peggy Lewis; Phyllis Lewis; Robert Lewis; Winifred McDade; Colin Morgan; Ira Morris; Eunice & Raymond Owen; Des Penhale; Michael Phelps; Pontardawe Community Council; Pontardawe Library staff; Gwen Pugh; Angela Rees; Swansea Reference Library; John Roberts; Linda Walkden; Lindsay Walker; Emlyn Williams; Huw Williams; Jackie Williams; Rachel Williams.